WHAT
IF YOU
PRAY?

Experiencing *the* Reality *of* Prayer

WHAT
IF YOU
PRAY?

Robert R. Cushman

WINEPRESS **WP** PUBLISHING

www.winepressbooks.com
1-877-421-READ (7323)

WinePress Publishing (PO Box 428, Enumclaw, WA 98022) functions only as book publisher. As such, the ultimate design, content, editorial accuracy, and views expressed or implied in this work are those of the author.

Unless otherwise noted, all Scriptures are taken from the *Holy Bible, New International Version®, NIV®*. Copyright © 1973, 1978, 1984 by the International Bible Society. Used by permission of Zondervan. All rights reserved.

Scripture references marked KJV are taken from the King James Version of the Bible.

ISBN 13: 978-1-57921-911-6
ISBN 10: 1-57921-911-X
Library of Congress Catalog Card Number: 2007925383

Printed in the United States of America.

TABLE OF CONTENTS

PREFACE

My thanks go to the many scholars, writers, pastors, co-workers, and other friends who have provided me with inspiration throughout my pastoral ministry.

Over the years I have trained my ear to listen to Truth. I am grateful to those people who have encouraged me with phone calls or e-mails, such as, "Bob this is a message that's challenged me." Or, "Here's a Scripture passage that's made a difference in my life. Read this." Or someone comes up to me and says, "Here, Bob, read this book. It's changed my life."

I know that they have been training their ears to hear God's Truth, applying that knowledge in their lives, and wanting it to have an effect on me as well. Their thoughts become embedded in mine, integral to my life experience.

I have been extremely blessed with the skills of my wife, Linda Cushman, and my mother, Helen Baker Cushman, in inventorying, organizing, and transcribing grainy audiocassette tapes and other media, and deciphering my handwritten drafts. They skillfully and faithfully helped to edit raw material into the readable format of this publication.

Chapter One

DID GOD TOUCH YOU?

While you're out in a boat, you learn to watch the weather. Thunderstorms, the wind blowing, or any kind of change in weather can be dangerous.

One Sunday, my wife and I had taken our children out on our boat to a place called Still Pond. As its name indicates, it was normally a very still and tranquil bit of water. You could pull the boat up and anchor into a sand bar. There the kids could jump off the boat and swim, and they'd be only waist deep. You didn't have to worry about them while they ran around the sand bar or over to the beach. We did watch them, and they were wearing life jackets, but we didn't have to be concerned about them being in water over their heads.

That day the weather had been forecast as calm and sunny. Around 6 o'clock, I was below deck when I noticed the newspaper was starting to blow away. I said, "Adam, grab the newspaper!" He was having difficulty grabbing it. I ran up topside and found the wind was blowing and had picked up to about

15 or 20 miles an hour. The boats near us were having some difficulty. We started to bounce around. Our towels were blowing away. We were grabbing everything as the wind was getting worse by the minute.

All of a sudden, the white caps started to appear. From then on, there we were, all night long, bouncing around in two and three foot waves, with all of our security at the end of a half-inch nylon line that ran out to an anchor.

I didn't sleep much that night. In a situation like that you fall asleep, then you jerk yourself awake to make sure you're not drifting into somebody else or onto the beach or some other disaster. I prayed a lot, feeling the heavy responsibility for bringing my whole family into this dangerous situation. I could imagine the report, "Christians lost at sea, all drowned!"

That began a week of terrible weather. Five days of dark clouds and rain followed that windy Sunday night. However, we survived, and on Friday morning we were able to pull into Havre de Grace, a town that has a public park with piers where we could dock our boat, and where we spent the night.

On Saturday morning, which was still dark and gloomy, when I was tinkering with the boat, I suddenly felt a sensation of warmth on my back. As I turned around, I could see the clouds starting to separate. There was the sun, and there was the blue sky! Streams of light were shooting down. The bay lit up. Other people who were near us came out of their boats, and we called out to each other, "Can you believe it? Look! It's finally sunshine! After five days!"

The sun was finally coming out, and as the clouds parted, it was as though God were drawing a curtain, pushing aside those thick clouds.

As my wife and I stood there, we said, "It's sunny, let's go! Let's get on our way!"

At that moment, I could only worship the Lord, overwhelmed with the greatness of his creation, and how he can turn darkness into light like that. Maybe it was because we had been living under dark clouds for so long that the sunshine appeared so especially brilliant. You could say I was having a worship service at that moment.

When God touches us in that way, we are overwhelmed with the greatness of his power, compassion, wisdom, and the greatness of the transformation that he can perform in each of our lives. When he ambushes us like that, we experience that certain knowledge of his greatness.

At such a time we also feel very small, insignificant, and vulnerable. All we can do, all we want to do, is fall down, worship, and pray. It's an amazing moment.

God will reach down and touch us each individually, and as our spirits rejoice, we will discover that our lives have been in some way changed forever.

Chapter Two

ALWAYS ON: STARTING YOUR CONVERSATION WITH GOD

Keeping in touch with my children has greatly improved since I discovered text-messaging. One day my cell phone wouldn't receive any messages, though it would send them. After what seemed like hours with Cingular's tech support, we finally figured out that the problem had to do with a setting labeled "Always On" or "When Needed." The "When Needed" setting didn't work, so I switched it to "Always On." That was the setting that kept the connection always open.

That reminded me of our spiritual life, where we can have an "always on" connection with God. Wherever we are, wherever we're going, whatever event we're involved in, that connection can always be active. The apostle Paul says,

> Be joyful always; pray continually; give thanks in all circumstances, for this is God's will for you in Christ Jesus.
> —1 Thessalonians 5:16

How do we "pray continually?" Do we become monks in cubicles, in constant prayer? We can communicate with God throughout the day, seeking God's leading for each moment. A friend of mine calls it "clicking in and out." As the phone rings, we pray, "Give me guidance." As we walk into a meeting, we can ask God for guidance before the business starts. In a difficult relationship with a fellow worker or with someone in authority, whatever the case is, throughout the day, we can quickly seek the Lord in prayer.

We can seek him in time of trouble, as the apostle Paul says,

> Rejoice in the Lord always. I will say it again: Rejoice! Let your gentleness be evident to all. The Lord is near. Do not be anxious about anything, but in everything, by prayer and petition, with thanksgiving, present your requests to God. (If we do that) . . . the peace of God, which transcends all understanding, will guard your hearts and your minds in Christ Jesus.
> —Philippians 4:4–7

God will give us a peace that passes all understanding. He will hold our hearts in his heart.

He says not to worry. It's so easy to worry, isn't it? It burns you out. But Paul says it's better to pray than to worry. When we're worried or concerned about something, it's difficult to pray, to get on our knees and surrender all to God. But that's exactly the time to pray without ceasing, because of the promise that the peace of God will guard you. Who wouldn't want the peace of God? That's a verse to keep in our memory.

As with those fleeting prayers for guidance, God hears our prayers of praise and thanksgiving. Throughout the day we can take moments to pause to look at creation around us. A beautiful day, or a rainy day, whatever it is, we have reason to give thanks that every moment we live is a gift from God.

God will help us walk through countless situations in all of our family relationships. Parents who are away from home during the day enter a new world as they come home in the evening, the world that their spouses and children have been experiencing. I know people who, before they enter their homes, pray, "Lord, guide me, because I'm walking into a totally different situation."

What about weekly? As we know, Scripture goes all the way back to the beginning of time, when God created the heavens and earth, and when God taught us to be aware of a certain pattern in life, one that he demonstrated for us. He created the heavens and earth and on the seventh day he rested. From that point forward, as he said to all humanity, "If you want to experience life at its fullest, you must take six days and rest on the seventh. And give honor to Me."

We translated that into the "Lord's Day," as it is in the New Testament, and now we celebrate that on Sunday, as a day of rest. Six days, and then one that's different, and if we follow that pattern it changes our lives.

The Christian college I attended was very conservative about observing the Sabbath, so conservative that they permitted no tests on either Monday morning or afternoon so that students would not spend Sunday cramming for tests. They would encourage the students to do nothing on Sunday except ministry or going to church.

That practice of giving one full day to the Lord is almost lost today. We've narrowed it down to one hour or less, depending on whether or not we go to church. Could we change our lives so that one day a week would be radically different?

Later we'll consider additional ways to open our communication lines with God. A process takes place, after we build a relationship with God, whereby we always have communication with him.

Chapter Three

HOW'S YOUR ATTITUDE?

I feel like my prayers are bouncing off the ceiling."

"Must we say 'amen' at the end of a prayer?"

"Should we dress in a certain way?"

"Is a certain posture recommended?"

"Is it better to be on top of a mountain, or is a valley all right?"

"How about our tone of voice?"

"Should there be a special sequence of words, or a certain eloquence, in order for God to listen to us?"

Let's define the attitude that we bring to prayer. When you're building a relationship with someone, what's the most important element in that process ?

When a couple falls in love, they usually say to each other, "Let's make sure that we're always honest with each other." For a relationship or friendship to be authentic, we want honesty.

The same thing is true in our relationship with God. For good communication with God, there must be honesty. He knows it all anyway, so why hold it back? What's the point of not telling him exactly how you feel? He already knows what you're thinking.

How do you think the first verse in Psalm 22 was spoken? In what tone of voice? Did David speak in quiet, courteous tones?

> My God, my God, why have you forsaken me?
>
> —Psalm 22:1

Or do you think he shouted in anger and desperation,

MY GOD, MY GOD, WHY HAVE YOU FORSAKEN ME?

In his anger, David was thinking, "Where's my salvation? Why have you done this to me?"

Have you ever scolded God? Isn't it irreverent to talk to God like that?

I don't think so.

If you're going to be honest about the pain in your life, the things that you're experiencing day to day, you must have those kinds of prayers with God. Sometimes we hold back saying, "I can't talk to God like that."

Sure you can.

If you're going to be honest with him, isn't it the same as if you're having an honest conversation with someone who's close to you? Or haven't you had those kinds of conversations, on those levels?

Then there are those times when we can be honest with God in expressing our joy and gladness. In the twenty-third Psalm, the same David says,

> The Lord is my shepherd, I shall not be in want.
>
> —Psalm 23:1

Here he's talking about the compassion and the love that he sees in God. How many times have you stopped to do that? You can remember a day when the sun was shining and the temperature was just perfect, an absolutely great day. Everyone felt it. On days like that have you stopped to say, "God, what a great day! I love it. I'm loving what's going on. I love the air. I love everything about this. It's just perfect. I sense you all around me."

It often happens, when something completely wonderful happens in our lives, that we get so busy with how wonderful it is, we never remember to thank God.

When something goes wrong, our knee-jerk reaction is to appeal to God. But, equally so, if we are going to be honest with God, we also need to thank him for our blessings, on a regular basis. That's communication.

Jesus tells us, "Don't give up." He tells a rather strange parable about a woman to whom something horrible had happened. She felt she had been misjudged or cheated in some way. She appealed to a judge for justice. The judge wouldn't hear her. She went back to him again and again to the point where she was standing in his office, sleeping there, driving him to distraction. Jesus also made the point that the judge was a difficult individual to start with.

> . . . who neither feared God nor cared about
> men.
>
> —Luke 18:2

Finally the judge, to get rid of her, granted her request. In concluding the parable, Jesus says, "How much more will God do for you?" Every one listening said, "What? God's going to answer our request to get us off his back?"

No. Jesus' point was that if the best response the judge could give is, "Get rid of this woman and give me some peace," our loving, heavenly Father, who is going to grant your request, is unimaginably beyond that. God is actively wanting to respond to you, and certainly not simply to be rid of you, to yield to your persistence.

In the Sermon on the Mount, Jesus talks about the power of prayer.

> Ask and it will be given to you; seek and you
> will find; knock and the door will be opened
> to you. For everyone who asks receives; he who
> seeks finds; and to him who knocks, the door
> will be opened.
>
> —Matthew 7:7–8

There's a promise. If you knock, if you seek, God will answer. God is always answering prayers. Sometimes you may not like his answer, but you prayed, and you received an answer.

Did you ever pray for patience? If you pray for patience, watch what happens. You'll learn patience.

Jesus told the parable about a Pharisee and his prayer. From a Jewish perspective, it was a very good prayer. Everything about the prayer was right, including the way the Pharisee postured himself, in humility, and the words he used. Some interpret the Pharisee's conduct as prideful, but the point is that he was correct, following all the aspects of prayer as they were perceived at that time.

Meanwhile, as Jesus told it, a tax collector was nearby, saying his prayers. In that time, tax collectors were known for corruption and for evil procedures in their collection of taxes. Jesus tells us that this tax collector prayed,

> God, have mercy on me, a sinner.
> —Luke 18:13

Then Jesus startled everyone when he said the tax collector went away "justified." Anyone hearing the story had trouble believing it. "What? How could the tax man go away justified? He didn't pray right. He's a miserable sinner."

Try having a relationship with someone who thinks that he or she is "somebody." It doesn't happen. Humility is an important aspect of prayer. If you come before God without humility, in an attitude of pride, you just might find your prayers bouncing off the ceiling.

Chapter Four

JUST SPEAK

How important is eloquence? I've heard some of the most eloquent prayers—especially from television preachers, or if you turn on C-Span and catch the prayer to open the Senate. I've thought, "Wow, that's pretty good. Carefully worded."

Do you think God cares? In corporate prayer, when an eloquent prayer is spoken aloud in front of an audience, the audience may well be edified by the speaker's words. It's different with personal prayer, between you and God.

What if, when the phone rings, you pick it up and hear the voice of a friend whom you haven't talked to in a long time, but the connection isn't good. Would you say, "Hey, call me back later when the connection is better. I can't talk to you now. I can't hear what you say." Would you say that?

Or, "When your English is a little better, then call me back."

Do you think God cares about our language or whether or not there's static on the line? He doesn't care!

On the occasions when I've had the opportunity to be with people who come to know Christ for the very first time, and we ask them to pray, sometimes they'll pray a simple prayer such as, "Hey God, it's me, Joe. Thanks." That's as meaningful to God as the most eloquent prayer that anyone could compose. The honesty needs to be there, not eloquence, not the way you phrase your words. It's just being straight up.

Do we need to speak when we pray? No, our prayers don't have to be spoken. God knows whatever is on your heart, so turn it over to him in whatever way works for you. Write it out, pray it silently, or speak it out loud. You may prefer to pray right on your laptop. Or you could come into the office early, write out a prayer on your computer, and save it as your prayer for the day. You could write a prayer on a Blackberry, if you have one. Those who are communicating with God, trusting in him, will find new strength.

> . . . those who hope in the Lord
>   will renew their strength.
> They will soar on wings like eagles;
>   they will run and not grow weary.
>   —Isaiah 40:31

The Bible gives quite a bit of information on how we should pray. The disciples asked Jesus, "How do we do this thing? How do we pray?" Without hesitation, he gave them a practical example.

Think of that very simple prayer, the one we call the "Lord's Prayer," found in Matthew 6:9–13.

Our Father who art in heaven . . .

That's saying, "Let's make sure we recognize who he is, the God of the universe."

Hallowed be thy name.

God is a holy, just God. Jesus goes on—each phrase in the prayer has so much meaning. He says,

Thy Kingdom come.

Yes, we want to see God's will done on earth as it is in heaven. That's our goal. We all want to advance God's Kingdom. We want to see God bless the whole world. That's from God's heart, that the whole world would be blessed, that he would have a relationship with every single person.

Then he reminds us of the most important thing, the breakdown of relationships, and the aspect of forgiveness. You can't love if you can't forgive.

Our daily bread . . .

What are the basic needs that God provides us? Food, clothing, shelter. God says, "I've got that covered." Why do we pray before a meal? Just acknowledging again the fact that everything we have is a gift from him.

This simple prayer puts our relationship with God into perspective, containing, as it does, key elements of our faith. The disciples asked how to pray, and God gave them that simple prayer.

We all want to know what God's will is for our lives. Two great verses, 3 and 4, in Psalm 37 say,

Trust in the Lord and do good;
    dwell in the land and enjoy safe pasture.
Delight yourself in the Lord
    and he will give you the desires of your heart.

—Psalm 37:3–4

Take delight in God and he will give you the desires of your heart! What a wonderful statement! Yes, God has a way of changing our hearts through communication, through a relationship with him. He gives us the desires of our hearts.

Often our human hearts lead us astray, but when we're in communication with God, he has his way of transforming our hearts into his heart and bringing us his peace that passes all understanding. The God who loves us more than we can imagine is willing to pour out blessing on our lives—but it begins with a relationship.

Chapter Five

HELPS AND MECHANICS

The Empty Chair

Of course our prayers are not bouncing off the ceiling. However, if you feel that's happening, you might like to use a practical device that some people have found helpful.

Try placing a chair in front of you as you pray. For some reason this helps some people to focus and to pray as though Jesus is in the chair, and they are speaking to him. Prayers bouncing off the ceiling? No. When you approach him, God hears, and he's listening.

The Time of Day

Morning or evening? Consistency, an important factor in achieving that relationship, requires discipline on our part. This means setting aside some time every day to pray.

The evening can be a very blessed time, including just before falling asleep, when the last thought on our minds is a prayer. Better yet, for most of us, is the morning, when we're awake, alert, and thinking about the whole day in front of us.

Speaking of morning prayer, the great Christian scholar, Dietrich Bonhoeffer, put it this way, "The Scriptures, moreover, tell us that the first thought and the first word of the day belong to God: 'My voice shalt thou hear in the morning, O Lord; in the morning will I direct my prayer unto thee.' (Ps. 5:3). . . . Therefore, at the beginning of the day, let all distraction and empty talk be silenced, and let the first thought and the first word belong to him to whom our whole life belongs."[1]

About evening prayer he has this to say, "When can we have any deeper sense of God's power and working than in the hour when our hands lay down their work and we commit ourselves to the hands of God? When are we more ready for the prayer of blessing, peace, and preservation than the time when our own activity ceases? When we grow weary, God does his work. 'Behold, he that keepeth Israel shall neither slumber nor sleep' (Ps. 121:4). . . . But over the night and over the day stands the word of the Psalter: 'The day is thine, the night also is thine (Ps. 74:16).'"[2]

For those who are not accustomed to consistent prayer, five minutes is a reasonable starting point, a small bit of time that we rush by during any day without a thought.

A-C-T-S

Another practical little aid to prayer, often useful for people who haven't been in the habit of personal prayer and don't quite know where to begin, is to remember the four letters A-C-T-S.

The first letter stands for Adoration. Adoration is worship, praising God. Instead of starting out with all the things we need God to do for us, we can start our prayer with adoration, meditating on how wonderful he is, perhaps with creation as a good place to start, then going on to the wonderful things we see around us, praising and adoring him.

Nothing special about any of us grants God's grace and favor to us. We are all sinners, and only through the grace of God do we have a relationship with him. It's all about him. He loved us with more love than we can ever imagine. Because of his passion for us, and for all humanity, he gave his life for us. Praising and adoring him in response to his love and sacrifice, brings our relationship with him into perspective.

The letter "C" stands for Confession. Confession is the opportunity to come clean, the honesty element of a relationship. We can pray that God will show us where we have failed.

By praying in those terms, sometimes those things we skip, or didn't see, come flooding to the surface. If the relationship between you and someone else is broken, or if something else in that relationship isn't right, then the communication between you is broken. But an opportunity will open up to get things right. Jesus said to settle disagreements and forgive one another.

If we confess our sins, God, who is faithful and just, will forgive our sins and cleanse us from all unrighteousness. Who wouldn't want to be cleansed from all unrighteousness? That's the confession aspect of prayer.

Our "T" stands for Thanksgiving, thanking God for all our blessings. Every good and wonderful gift that comes our way is from God. Our prayer might include all the things we have to be thankful for—our children, our family, our life, our health.

Being thankful people, and having thankfulness as a regular part of our prayers, changes us. The more we are thankful for the things in our lives, the more we become thankful as we recognize those wonderful blessings in our lives.

Finally, the "S," the last capital letter in our acrostic, represents Supplication. "God, I need your help." "Lord, hear my prayer." That's our shopping list. God wants to hear those needs and wants to respond to them. We pray for our own needs and those of others.

Some years ago I began to make a special point of asking people if I could pray for them. I'd say, "Can I pray for you?" You might think their response would be, "Not on your life will you pray for me, no way, Cushman." No, they don't say that. They say, "Yes, great. You want to pray for me? Super."

When someone tells me something that's on his or her mind, I will always pray for that person and for those concerns. People seem grateful when I follow up with them to tell them I prayed for them. Sometimes, afterwards, they ask me if I've been praying for them. Or they say, "I've got another one for you. Pray for this." And I will pray, not as a token gesture, but in depth and sincerity when our supplication is in line with God's commandments.

I find that no matter what their religious background, or what's going on, people in the community at large are always interested in somebody praying for them.

So we have ACTS—Adoration, Confession, Thanksgiving, and Supplication. It's easy. Try it.

Chapter Six

LISTEN, THAT WAS HIS VOICE

It's a personality fault of mine to be always in a hurry. To help offset that, I drive the oldest vehicle I can get my hands on, so I'll be forced to drive slowly.

One irate policeman gave me a memorable speeding ticket some years ago when I was coming home from a church meeting. Our friends, Steve and Catherine, were visiting us from Canada while we were helping them with an adoption. It was important for them, along with my wife, Linda, to be at the courthouse at a certain time, so I had promised to be back in time to baby-sit our children.

Earlier in the day I had reminded myself to be careful not to be late, not to risk getting a speeding ticket, or Steve and Catherine would be late for the most important day of their lives.

Yet, there I was, running late, foot on the pedal, almost airborne in my haste, two blocks from my house, just as a policeman was coming the other direction.

"Oh, no!" I thought as I saw him turn around. "They can still make it if I can just get to the driveway, then they can leave."

I managed to fly into my driveway, with the police car right in there after me.

Standing there were Linda, Steve and Catherine, my kids, and some neighbors. I jumped out of the car, told them to go, "I'll take care of this."

The policeman was not happy.

That was just one of several speeding tickets that I confess to having earned.

It's a story about ignoring my own better judgment, not planning more time, and not going more slowly, so that I could have saved myself a ticket and that huge fine.

That's something like the way it is when we hear God's voice but don't pay attention. He speaks, but we block out the reality of his presence beside and within us, so that we close our hearts, eyes, and ears to his voice, letting our desire of the moment take over.

A passage from Proverbs illustrates this:

> Trust in the Lord with all your heart
> and lean not on your own understanding;
> in all your ways acknowledge him,
> and he will make your paths straight.
> —Proverbs 3:5–6

Paraphrased, that timeless passage reads, "Trust God completely. Don't try to figure it all out by yourself. Listen for God's voice. He'll give you the help you need and keep you from going astray." If you listen to God for just five minutes, don't be surprised if you hear God say something—perhaps about what's on your mind, or something completely unexpected.

The Still, Small Voice

Think of Elijah. Elijah was challenged to go and stand before God on a mountain. He was supposed to listen for God. So, as he was standing on the mountain, a hurricane blew by that he thought surely must be God. He listened but God wasn't in the hurricane.

Then, as Scripture says, an earthquake shook the mountain, but God wasn't there. Elijah didn't hear God in the earthquake.

When a mighty fire came next, Elijah thought that would have to be God. He waited and listened, but God wasn't in the fire.

Finally, just sitting there, he heard a "still small voice" (KJV), "a gentle whisper," (1 Kings 19:12 NIV). It was God, speaking to him.

I've found that, throughout the course of my walk with God, he often speaks in that still, small voice.

We won't hear him if we're waiting for a loud voice, a high definition, DVD-quality sound. We won't hear him when we're so busy that we're not quiet enough to listen to God.

The time to hear him is when we've set aside a few minutes of silence and said, "God, speak to me." Just listen. Stop talking. As we do so, we begin to recognize God's voice and respond to it.

That's not to say that he doesn't occasionally speak in high definition. I haven't personally heard him that way, but I know people who have. When he does, it's a huge wake-up call.

Getting It the Hard Way

Noah is an interesting person who listened to God. He built that big ship in his backyard as God had told him to do. What made God's request seem so bizarre was that no one had seen a flood. They were not accustomed to rain. If God has ever spoken to you to do something very unusual, you'll know how Noah felt.

God has asked many people to take some kind of action which didn't seem to make sense at the moment. Yet, when you look back over the course of human history, you'll realize that many people whose lives have been influential were those who responded to God's words to do something unusual.

Those who failed to listen, like Noah's neighbors and fellow countrymen, learned their lesson too late.

How Do We Know It's God?

How do we determine the will of God, what God is calling us to do?

Someone said to me, "I feel God has called me to the mission field."

"So why wouldn't you go?" I asked.

"Well, my husband doesn't want me to go."

"God isn't asking you to break up your marriage. He isn't calling you if your husband doesn't want you to go."

The Scripture tells us, and I think it's safe to say, that God will never lead us to do something that is in conflict with what his own word says. Yes, possibly the command may seem bizarre, but he will not lead us to violate the Word of God as revealed either in what is directly said or what is implied in the Bible.

Once we are willing to say "yes" to God, when we follow through with what he tells us to do, we find ourselves doing it with passion and commitment. It becomes the desire of our heart. There's nothing else in the world that we want to do more than that.

If we're willing to listen, God will speak. Whatever he says, we must listen to him. God wants more than anything else to be in a relationship with us and that we would be open to his voice. Then all we need to say is, "Give me the strength to respond to you."

Chapter Seven

IS THERE HEALING FOR US THROUGH PRAYER?

Healers on television are fascinating to watch. They'll say something like, "Is someone out there unable to hear out of your left ear since you were a child?" Someone will raise a hand. If it's a woman, she'll come up front, the healer puts his hand on her, and he prays for her. Whoa! She falls down backwards and is healed, or it seems so. I think some of them do get healed.

I encouraged a friend in Canada to attend a certain church service that held healing services. She attended a service, was healed, and continued in remission for several years until the tumor again became active. We know that prayer has a direct connection to healing. I believe that God heals.

Studies on the subject of healing find no consistent data to document that one person can consistently heal over and over again. Tests have shown where one group of sick people was prayed for, and another group was not. Results showed that the group that was prayed for did better than the test group that was not prayed for. Those doing the praying would not necessarily be Christians, or even religious people.

The book of James speaks to the question, "Is there really healing for us today?"

> Is any one of you in trouble? He should pray. Is anyone happy? Let him sing songs of praise. Is any one of you sick? He should call the elders of the church to pray over him and anoint him with oil in the name of the Lord. And the prayer offered in faith will make the sick person well; the Lord will raise him up. If he has sinned, he will be forgiven. Therefore confess your sins to each other and pray for each other so that you may be healed. The prayer of a righteous man is powerful and effective.
>
> —James 5:13–16

James means that in the case of any illness—mental, physical, or spiritual—you have the privilege of calling the church elders to come together and pray for you, and if that prayer is offered in faith, you will be healed.

In the churches I have been involved in, we have believed that God provides healing, and we would, if requested, pray for people after the service or at another appointed time.

As to watching healing services on television, there must be something about our human nature that likes to see good happen to someone in trouble. Those television evangelists can create an audience because they are doing something good for someone in a bad situation. It does appear that God has gifted some people and ministries for healing.

Most of the time when Christ healed people, it was quietly and off to the side. He healed those lepers and told them not to tell anyone else. Only on a couple of occasions was it a public event, and then only after he was pressured into it or had been set up to do it. Nobody saw it or knew about it except that individual and the disciples who were with him at the time. Allowing the sick person some privacy was typical of the compassion of Jesus. If we're sick or suffering, the last place we want to be is center stage.

So, in my experience, when we pray for people, it's done in private, without making a big deal about it. In fact, our last comment before they leave is that if they get healed, we would like to know. We tell them, "We won't make a public announcement, but if you would just get back to those of us who prayed for you, we would like to know what happened."

I have seen some amazing answers to prayer. This is my testimony, and you can make of it what you wish. There was a time when a man asked us to pray for him. His business was in sewing fabrics to make seat cushions. Somehow he had managed to cut his arm very severely. As I looked at the nasty gash I was thinking, "He should go to the hospital. This is more than we can pray for." However, we called together the elders, and we prayed for him.

A couple of days later, he came back, put his arm out, and showed us that there was just a mark on his arm. The injury should have had stitches, but it was just gone.

Another time, a man came and asked us to pray for him. He had been diagnosed with a number of tumors on his intestines. We prayed for him and for the next step, which was to be pre-op surgery a couple of days later. He went in for those tests, was tested thoroughly, and received the report that nothing at all was wrong with him. He came back to us and said, "I've been healed."

In none of these situations when we prayed did I sense light coming into the room. Nobody fell over backwards. Neither I nor anyone else felt an unusual filling of the Holy Spirit. Each time we prayed for anyone who was healed, it was the same as any other time.

A gentleman came to us who had been diagnosed with hardening of arteries and was scheduled for bypass surgery. We prayed for him. When he went for his final test right before surgery, they couldn't find anything wrong with him. He told us, "My heart is as good as it was when I was seventeen."

No one could take credit for it. We were there, and we had prayed for him. That was all we did.

Another time, a woman came and asked us to pray for her. She had been bipolar for a long time, taking all kinds of medication. She told us, "I really feel that God could heal me."

Without any special conviction, I thought, "OK." After we prayed for her, she said, "I'm going to stop taking my medication."

I said, "Whoa! Don't stop taking your medication. I don't know if I have that much faith. I prayed for you, and I believe God can heal you." We met with her husband, explained the situation to him, and received his approval. She stopped taking that medication and never took it again. She was healed. She knew she was healed.

One more true story: A fellow came to us after the service one Sunday, a salesman who traveled quite a bit. He said to me that he just hadn't been feeling well. He didn't seem to have any energy, though he had been to the doctor. "I think God is calling me here by faith to have you pray for me," he said. He was to fly to India the next morning.

We gathered some elders around him and prayed for him. We prayed that people around him would have wisdom to diagnose his problem, and that God would use the physicians to bring healing. After we prayed, he went home and, as he walked in the front door, his wife said, "I think you should go and get an X-ray."

He said, "For what?" But she said she didn't know, the idea had just popped into her head. To humor her, he went back to his doctor and had an X-ray done. The doctor, who was surprised that he requested an X-ray, was even more surprised to find a hole in his patient's lung. "You would have had a collapsed lung," he said. "And what would they have done for you in the air at 35,000 feet? If you had flown, it would have killed you."

That was God's healing.

In probably the most amazing healing in my experience, I received a call from the wife of a church member who had been admitted to the hospital. She, herself, was a doctor at the hospital. She told us, "He's in really bad shape. We don't know what's wrong with him." The plain facts were that he was bleeding to death, and no one knew the cause of the bleeding.

A group of us drove up to the hospital and walked into his room, which was filled with all kinds of high tech officials and doctor friends trying to figure out what was wrong. The patient appeared to be dying, about to step over into eternity, absolutely white, barely breathing.

His wife pushed everyone away saying, "The pastors are here, they are going to pray for him." We laid hands on him, anointed him with oil, prayed for him, and left. I can remember thinking to myself as we went down in the elevator, "We're going to have a funeral. This guy is not going to make it."

We came back to church and left from there for our separate homes. As I pulled into my driveway, my wife came running out the front door.

She said, "Did you hear, did you hear?" This was before everyone had cell phones. I said, "No, what happened?"

She said, "He's healed. He's sitting up in the chair."

I said, "You've got to be kidding me. Are we talking about the same person?"

I rushed back to the hospital, and, as I walked in, there he was, sitting in his chair, completely healed.

There's a funny part to this. I could hear his wife over in the corner, insisting to the other doctors that they weren't to do surgery. They wanted to cut him open to find out why he was healed. She was over there saying they weren't to cut her husband open.

At times when I have shared these accounts with people, others have told me even more amazing stories about how God had healed them.

So I really do believe in healing. I have seen it with my own eyes. I can't take credit for it. Scripture tells us to draw all the elders together, and someone would have the faith to believe that God would bring healing.

People's mental issues, depression, bi-polarism—we've prayed for all kinds of conditions and in many cases have seen healing. In just as many cases we haven't seen any healing. I've prayed for people and then done their funerals.

According to James, the apostle, for healing to take place, certain conditions should be met. James says to call the elders together. It would be difficult to call a group of elders together to pray for us if we are not connected to a nearby church. James was assuming that his readers were connected with a community of believers.

If we are not connected to a local church or part of a fellowship, then who would we call? If someone walked into a Christian church, asked if it had elders, and wished to follow the Biblical pattern, the pastors or clergy probably wouldn't require a membership certificate, and would be willing to pray for him or her. Yet the teaching of James implies that, for our own well being, we should be able to say, "These are my elders. This is my church." We might take it a step further and say that our prayers, and our opportunity for others to pray for us, could be greatly hindered if we haven't followed that pattern.

The apostle Paul, in his letter to the Ephesians, speaks to this point. He refers to the congregation, the Christian community, with the precisely descriptive term, the "body of Christ."

> . . . to prepare God's people for works of service, so that the body of Christ may be built up until we all reach unity in the faith and in the knowledge of the Son of God and become mature, attaining to the whole measure of the fullness of Christ.
>
> —Ephesians 4:12–13

Paul is saying that it's impossible for us to experience maturity in Christ, or even to experience the fullness of Christ, apart from the context of community. We are using our gifts in connection with others as they use theirs.

On the subject of healing, James makes a second point—that we should have enough faith to ask someone to pray for us.

Sometimes we would get the call, "My wife told me I had to call you."

I'd say, "OK, great, what are you calling for?"

"I'd like to have you guys pray for me."

"Absolutely, let's do it Sunday right after the service. We'll make it happen."

Sometimes I'd get a report as someone was walking out the church door, "I'm going for surgery on Tuesday."

I'd say, "Did you think about having anybody pray for you?"

"Oh yeah, I got busy and didn't think about it."

I've had people say to me, "You're just like us. What's the difference between you and me? I can pray for myself."

We must have faith to pray. It takes a certain amount of boldness. The healing sometimes happens before the elders even walk in the room. At such times, people had faith enough to follow the Biblical teaching. People were already healed before our elders arrived at the hospital.

There is indeed a time and a place for personal prayer for our own healing if our illness is mental, physical, or spiritual. Spiritual? When we feel as though we're a million miles from God, there's that simple prayer: "God, how are we doing? It feels as though you're a million miles away, and I can't get back connected with you."

Life is a gift. Every moment of every day is another gift from God. No guarantees come with this gift. God granted us the privilege to live. But through his love and compassion, he desires to bring healing.

The prayer for healing requires honesty. James brings out the point that we are to be honest before God, to confess our sins, to say it like it is. Some of our illnesses come on us because of the way we live, the stresses we are under, and unhealthy living habits. We go through our lives burdened with unconfessed sin, laden with guilt within us, all building up physical problems.

When I think of an honest prayer, I think of Christ in the Garden of Gethsemane, right before he takes the sins of the whole world on his shoulders. He prays with such anxiety before God that, as the Bible says, he sweats blood. What is he praying?

> Going a little farther, he fell with his face to the
> ground and prayed, "My Father, if it is pos

sible, may this cup be taken from me. Yet not as
I will, but as you will.

—Matthew 26:39

Jesus is thinking, "If there's another way to do this deal and save humanity, if you have option two, I would love for that to go through. I don't want to do this. Is there some other way?"

But then what does he say? "Whatever your call, I'm going to do it." He presses through, and the God of the universe takes the sin of the whole world on his shoulders. But he was honest, wasn't he? That was real honesty before God.

A healing process takes place in being able to say to a close Christian friend whom we can trust, "Hey look, this is my life today. This is where I blew it."

In the same way, we can speak to the Lord. The apostle Paul reminds us to pray about anything, to bring everything before him in honesty. God's grace will be sufficient for us.

Do not be anxious about anything, but in everything, by prayer and petition, with thanksgiving, present your requests to God.

—Philippians 4:6

Chapter Eight

WHEN LEADINGS CHANGE OUR LIVES

For most of my life, I have sensed God's leading and directing in some very profound ways. When I was twenty-two, I clearly knew that God was calling me into full-time ministry with my wife, Linda. We didn't know what kind of ministry it would be, perhaps the missionary field, only that we were to serve the Lord full time.

Off we went to seminary, then to our first church—Mountainside Gospel Chapel, in Mountainside, New Jersey. Four years later came God's call to Princeton Alliance Church, New Jersey. The latter move changed my life more than anything up to that time.

The course and direction of our lives can be changed as we follow God's leadings and promptings, in both large and small ways.

Just Stopping By

One Friday, on my way home after a busy afternoon, I experienced a leading to call on one of our Rotary members, something I would not normally do.

I pleaded, "Lord, I've had a real busy afternoon. This is not a good time."

But the leading was unmistakable, so I turned the car around. On my way over to this man's office, I wondered, "What am I going to tell him? What would he think if I were to say, 'Sorry to bother you, but I just had a leading.' Lord, I hope you've got this thing under control."

I pulled into the parking lot, and as I walked into the reception area, there he was, standing in the hallway. My heart sank. "Here I am, and this doesn't make sense."

"Hey, Cushman!"

"Hey, how're you doing?"

"What are you doing?"

"I came by to see you."

"Oh, man, great! Come in here to my office."

We walked into his office, and, as soon as he closed the door, he began to tell me how an employee had taken off with a great deal of the company's money. After we talked, he said, "I'm so glad you came by. It's made a difference to me. I think I can deal with it."

Driving home, I marveled, "Six billion people in the world, and God looks down and sees this person who needs some help. He looks at me, says, 'Your schedule doesn't matter,' and puts the two of us together!"

We all receive leadings, and not always, as in this case, do they take us out of our way. They may come when we're in the grocery store or at a business meeting or in some other crowded room. We'll encounter someone we haven't seen in a while and say, "How are you?" Instead of hearing the usual, "Fine, thanks," we find ourselves listening longer than we had planned, with compassion and preferably without topping the story with one of our own.

When Green Meant Wait

Here in New Jersey we have some exotic intersections. At a busy intersection in South Brunswick, where a local road crosses U.S. Route One, a button on the traffic pole can supposedly control the light, as a back-up in case the signal doesn't work. I've seen people get out of their cars and push that button to change the light. I don't know if it works, but it may have helped to pass the time, as the wait at that intersection always seems endless.

The green light permits a sharp turn across the highway to the southbound lane. During the few seconds after the change from red to green and back to red again, there's hardly a split second to look up and down the highway before you have the chance to step on the gas and cross over to the far right-hand lane.

One day, late for an appointment, I was in front, sitting there at the red light, waiting and watching. Just as the light turned green, I was all set to step on the gas and dash across, when a leading came, "Don't go."

I thought, "Oh, no! What's this? Not to move?"

The driver behind me blew his horn.

At that second—it all happened in a second—a tractor-trailer charged through the red light. I must have turned white, while the driver behind me also looked shaken.

After we came through that intersection, I was overwhelmed with the realization of what had just happened.

An Answered Call

It was 10:30 at night, and I was at home, when a phone call came from a church member, Yvonne.

"Bob, I just got a call from my daughter in California. Her friend is on business in upstate New York and is staying in a motel. She's pregnant, bleeding, just went to the emergency room. The doctor told her to go back and rest in her hotel room. What should I do?"

I said, "It's 10:30 at night. The doctors have released her, so she should be OK till morning. Can't this wait till then?"

But Yvonne had a strong leading. She hung up the phone, figured out where this girl was, jumped in her car, and drove the three or four hours. Arriving at about 3 a.m., she picked up the young woman, and drove her to Princeton. The next morning, she called, "Where do I take this girl?"

Our church members included several fine physicians, and in short time she was in good hands. It turned out that this young woman had a tubular pregnancy and required emergency surgery. In awe I thought, "Yvonne, if you had listened to me and not listened to God, this would not have had a happy ending." God connected one woman, out of six billion people in the world, with someone in need of help.

Is It from God?

We may ask how we know our leadings are from God. First, leadings will always be in conformity to God's Word. For example, an individual gets hold of a gun, shoots someone, and says, "God told me to do it!" How do we know that he's not lying? We know he's lying or deranged, because God will never give a leading that is contrary to his very word. God's not going to ask you to do something he has forbidden us to do.

Secondly, it is always helpful to ask, "What would Jesus do if he were in a situation like this?"

A third point is to seek guidance. When we face a major decision, and we have a sense of leading, it's always helpful to seek out someone with a leadership role in our life. "What's your spin on this thing? How do you read this?"

Finally, does it fit our personality, the way that we've been wired up?

As an example, I've heard this illustration, and perhaps you've heard it too.

A man asked a counselor, "I think God is calling me to be a pastor. What do you think about this? Do you think this is God's leading?"

The counselor replied, "Do you like interpersonal relationships? Do you like lots of intense relationships?"

"No, I hate all that. I get very stressed dealing with all kinds of people."

"Well, do you like preaching? Do you like putting thirty hours of time into a message?"

"No, I'm not at all studious. That wouldn't work for me."

"Sorry, I don't think God's calling you to be a pastor."

So the four criteria are: Does the leading fit the Word of God? What would Jesus do? What do leaders around you, or your mentor, say? Does it fit who you are?

Could I Have More?

Christianity is all about a relationship with the living God, being in fellowship with him every day. In seeking that communication, we need some time each day to commune with God in prayer.

Many of us are extremely busy. When the alarm goes off, we wake up. Instantly our feet are on the floor, and we're off and running for the rest of the day. Yet we could pause for just a moment, when we first wake up, and before the light goes on, to say, "Lord, I want to do this day with you." Starting our day like that helps us to be open to many of God's leadings.

Many of us take it beyond that brief moment, by starting the morning with a longer devotional time to include prayer about our day ahead, about the people we will be working with, current events, our business deals, our families and friends. We might take time to read Bible passages, praying about them, making a simple request of God such as, "Lord, use me today to bring love, hope, and an opportunity to serve others. Show me yourself this morning. Reveal what I need to hear from you, from your Word."

Some of us have a prayer time in the evening—especially those who can't function in the morning. Morning, noon, or evening, whenever we spend that quiet time with God, we will receive leadings from him, as long as we understand that God wants to have a relationship with us and to build that relationship with us every day.

It's also helpful to memorize some Bible verses that apply to us. For example, for someone like myself who tends to be more hasty than compassionate, a good reminder is,

> Be kind and compassionate to one another, forgiving each other, just as in Christ God forgave you.
> —Ephesians 4:32

"OK, Lord, I'm trying."

Do we need to remind ourselves of our calling to love God and love others?

Jesus said,

> "'Love the Lord your God with all your heart and with all your soul and with all your mind.' This is the first and greatest commandment. And the second is like it: 'Love your neighbor as yourself.' All the Law and the Prophets hang on these two commandments."
> —Matthew 22:37–40

Do we need to keep a check on pride in our accomplishments, or those of our children and grandchildren?

> God opposes the proud
> but gives grace to the humble.
> —1 Peter 5:5

If we keep that verse in mind, the Holy Spirit will use it as a prompting.

> For it is by grace you have been saved, through faith—and this not from yourselves, it is the gift of God—not by works, so that no one can boast. For we are God's workmanship, created in Christ Jesus to do good works, which God prepared in advance for us to do.
>
> —Ephesians 2:8–10

Do we hold too tightly to earthly possessions?

> Do not store up for yourselves treasures on earth, where moth and rust destroy, and where thieves break in and steal. But store up for yourselves treasures in heaven, where moth and rust do not destroy, and where thieves do not break in and steal. For where your treasure is, there your heart will be also.
>
> —Matthew 6:19–21

If we seal these words of Jesus into our memories, from time to time the Holy Spirit will remind us of them so that eternal values become our priority.

Not all of us are helped by memorizing verses. Or, some of us may need different verses. If your essential personality already leads you to impart tenderness, compassion, and gentleness, you may need help in some other area, such as freedom from fear. The apostle Paul refers to boldness in the Lord.

> For God did not give us a spirit of timidity, but
> a spirit of power, of love and of self-discipline.
> —2 Timothy 1:7

Then, when you feel fearful, the Holy Spirit will bring that verse into memory, and you'll say, "Yes! I'm going to be bold for Christ."

Those are only examples, and not necessarily the verses that would apply to all or any of us, but when we've selected a half dozen verses that relate to what we want to see God doing in our lives, we will receive promptings and leadings that connect directly to them.

Then, as we say, "Yes, Lord, I'm going to do that," our relationship with God matures.

When we talk about leadings, the One who must receive the credit, the One whom we praise, is not the one who obeys the leading. The One we worship for his marvelous guidance to us is the One who gives the leading.

The very God who gives the leadings, Jesus Christ himself, is the very God who died on the Cross that we might have life abundantly, so that we might have a relationship with the living God every single moment of every single day.

Chapter Nine

DISCONNECT!

A sense of being disconnected from God may come some time after we have experienced his love, his guidance, and his transformation of our lives. We may have grown in our relationship with him, have loved being a part of a church family, and have believed that we are advancing the Kingdom through our tithes and offerings.

You may have walked through your day or week or year and left God far behind. You then find it's not always easy to reconnect immediately. I can identify with that. There have been days when I've found that I've totally disconnected from God. I've been doing my thing, busy with church, work, and my schedule. I don't know where God's been, but we haven't connected. The next day I have a harder time getting reconnected.

In hearing people say that for years, and as we consider the subject of prayer; how we connect with God; how God touches us; and how, when, and where we pray; I'm constantly reminded of the differences between us in our own unique, personal connection with God.

To identify our own uniqueness helps us to have a more consistent walk with Christ and to appreciate the diversities among us all.

When Being Alone Doesn't Work

Some of us have difficulty studying God's Word in isolation. If you're one of these people, you may find your mind wandering as you pray. In a worship environment, if you sit by yourself, you're uncomfortable, and feel a need to be with someone else.

In a Bible study, however, surrounded by other people, you're completely at ease and feel you could study the Bible all day long. In a prayer group with other people, your prayers flow as long as the situation requires. In a worship service, where you can sit with your friends, worship becomes alive for you.

Again, if you're involved in some task or service project where you find yourself serving all alone, that's drudgery. If you're in a team, your team spirit blooms, and you feel you're right where you belong.

A friend of mine realized he was in that category, knowing it was important to have quiet time with God every day and that he was not achieving it. "I can't do it," he said. "I get up in the morning to do it, and I can't seem to get connected."

I said, "Look, why don't you try something different? Try attending one of our men's Bible studies that meets in the morning?"

After he started meeting with a few other men during the early morning, he said, "That was the best thing that ever happened to me."

Two years later, he reported, "I get so connected to God by being with those guys, having them hold me accountable, talking about guy things, talking about planning service projects, and discussing the implication of the word on our lives, it carries me through the whole week."

Later we'll discuss solitude and how it's possible for even those who haven't yet been able to use solitude in their walk with Christ, to develop that as an aid to drawing close to God.

Facts First

If you seek answers through study of the Bible and of the roots of our Christian faith, a time will come when you will sense God's pleasure and empowerment on your life. When you have all your questions answered, and after you've wrestled with those answers intellectually, then your hearts, souls, and energies become fully engaged. Some of you are wired that way and have given yourselves to teaching ministries.

At one of the first churches I attended, the service started with three hymns and some prayers, all lasting not over ten minutes. Following that came a *click,* that could be heard all over the sanctuary—the sound of notebooks clicking open as we readied to embark, for the next 45 minutes, on an intellectual study of God's Word. These folks used scriptural information to connect to God. Scripture is probably the most common and effective way that we connect with God. Yet there is a warning—we need to be careful that we do not fall in love with the Bible instead of falling in love with Jesus.

A Closer Walk Through Service

Some of us reach fulfillment through service.

These people love to be a part of the work of loving their neighbors. They find their closeness to God through acts of service, both to the church and extending outward to the community at large. You may be one of these, or you may have found that this is your connection with God, without realizing it, and without having engaged in it. You may wonder, "Why is it that my Christianity seems to be up and down and all over the place?" Perhaps you've never taken this connection as a viable way to draw you closer to God.

During my thirty years of pastoral ministry, I have found that more people draw closer to God through this connection than any other.

Quiet Before God

Some of us flourish when we can be quiet before God, alone, with a Bible, a journal, or a good piece of literature, lost in contemplation of God's Word. We feel the need to tell how much Jesus cared about the poor and the suffering, and how the church should mirror Christ's heart.

Those who work in solitude often provide the inspiration for many church outreach ministries, and have been the authors of influential books on the Christian life, and of hymns and music familiar in Christian worship services. Yet, a word of caution to those who flourish in solitude with God: you will sometimes find yourselves drained when you're in a group. Too much fellowship, and your battery's quickly going dead. For the rest of us who do not have that meditative nature, let us cherish these folks and help them find whatever opportunity they need for privacy and solitude, whether in the course of congregational life, or in the family home.

Faith at 100 Miles an Hour

I love speed. If we're not doing something impossible apart from God then I'm not interested. I often find God right at the edge. In the early days of my pastoral ministry, it would often take a week of a two-week vacation just to slow down. Perhaps this is like you, tearing through life as fast as you can for the Kingdom of God. During the day, you may be heard invoking the name of God, "I need your help, need it a little bit more." At the end of the day you put your head on the pillow, exhausted.

People were amazed at the many different things Dwight L. Moody could do all at once. Founder of the Bible Institute that bears his name, Moody was involved in a variety of other ministries.

From what we know about the Methodist church, John Wesley was a "Kingdom maniac," seemingly going in five different directions at once, loving every minute of it.

George Whitfield, as we know from what we have heard of the Great Awakening, preached to the point of exhaustion.

People were amazed at Dr. A. B. Simpson, founder of the Christian and Missionary Alliance, a denomination in which I served as a pastor for many years. Simpson was another high energy, activist-type, who was sending missionaries overseas and producing newsletters, and had a training school, a college, a publishing company, even a restaurant that he was trying to run. The busier he was in Kingdom building, the closer to God he found himself.

Some of you are investing your activist tendencies in worldly paths. It may be that God is calling you to turn your energies toward his business. You will find yourself in a closer walk with him when you start to apply your energies in doing what God is doing and what God is about.

Through the Beauty of the Earth

For some of us a sunset or a sunrise can draw our hearts toward God.

The smell of a forest after a rain moves our hearts towards God's heart. We can be so close to God, whether it's the shore or the beach or watching a sunrise.

Some of us respond to God in our backyards, with fields of flowers, or with ferned grottos and shady nooks. They find themselves close to God, even in simple tasks like checking their tomato plants and pulling a few weeds.

A Closer Walk Through Music

Great music comes from God and leads our spirits toward him. With the invention of the iPod and MP3 players, those who find music as a way to hear God's voice are now truly blessed. My iPod holds over 4,000 songs, and often just the right song is just what I need to help me hear God's still voice.

Music draws many of us toward worship, to closeness to God, helping us to sense his presence.

Which Is Yours?

As we approach God in terms of who we are, we become like him, and we become his representatives, because he has called us to the wonderful task of partnering with him in loving the world.

Chapter Ten

WHEN THE GAME BOARD'S PUT AWAY

When I was about 8 or 9, our family would play Monopoly together in the living room. We would set up the board, and my sister, my father, my mother, and I would play in the evenings. The game would go on for days with the rules being, "Don't steal anybody's money, and don't knock the board." On a regular basis, being young, I would lose. They'd wipe me out, taking all my properties. Even though I owned a few hotels, I would be completely bankrupt, while my sister would look over and say, "Some day you'll learn to play the game."

After a while, I figured it out and started to win a few games. I can remember once when my mother went to the bank and brought home real money—ones, tens, twenties, and fifties. Playing with real money made the game more challenging. I can remember winning and how wonderful it felt. I beat them all, raked in everybody's hotels, wiped them out, cleaned up. They were bankrupt. I had won.

So I eventually learned how to play the game. I learned another lesson, and that is, in the end, it all goes back in the box. All the money went back to the bank. All the cards were stacked up and put back in the box. The hat and all the rest of it, with my little ship, went back in the box.

As we grow older, we learn that everything eventually goes back in the box.[3]

We live in an "all about me" world that projects an illusion that we can have it all. The illusion is that not only can we have it all, but also we should have it all, and we should not go through the pain of not having it all.

We may have a rewarding career, worldly acclaim, exceptional children, wonderful friends, and every kind of good fortune. Yet, Scripture clearly tells us, as we know from our own experience, that we can't have it all, all of the time. Scripture also tells us, in the words of Jesus, not to worry about what we're going to wear or where we're going to live or what we're going to own, and that God, in his love, will take care of what we need.

> But seek first his kingdom and his righteousness, and all these things will be given to you as well.
>
> —Matthew 6:33

How is it, that if we seek the Kingdom of God, all these things will be given to us? How can that happen?

Over the course of human history, as people have sought out God, they have discovered that, of all things in life, their relationship with God is the most important. At some point in their lives, a trial, a blessing, or whatever event caused them to wake up, turns their lives around and they say, "All my pursuit of success, material objects, fame, and fortune has not been worth it in light of my walk with Christ."

It all starts with a relationship with God. We human beings come to a point in our lives where we make a decision to follow Christ and to follow him first and foremost. It's a choice we make when we realize that our sin has separated us from God, but Christ has paid the price for that. So as the Gospel of John says,

> . . . to all who received him, to those who believed in his name, he gave the right to become children of God.
>
> —John 1:12

When we make that choice to receive Christ, we become a son or daughter of the King, a child of God. We become like him, in his heart of love and concern for all people, and we become his representatives to the world around us.

How is it possible to have the mind and heart of Christ? What do we do to make that happen? The process unfolds through spiritual discipline, developing a way of worship in walking with Christ, communicating with our Heavenly Father, that can help shape our hearts to be like His.

The apostle Paul discusses the concept of "spiritual exercise" or "spiritual training."

> Do you not know that in a race all the runners run, but only one gets the prize? Run in such a way as to get the prize. Everyone who competes

in the games goes into strict training. They do
it to get a crown that will not last; but we do it
to get a crown that will last forever.
—1 Corinthians 9:24–25

His point is that, obviously, try as hard as they may, people cannot win a race unless they have trained as runners. Using his illustration in comparison with our spiritual hearts, there's a difference between something that we try to do and something that we train to do. The way to become strong in our faith, to have the mind and heart of Christ, is by a certain discipline that we might call "training" or "exercise." This contrasts with simply taking a try at it once in a while, or with fitting Christianity in with all the other things that we're trying to do in our lives, as time permits.

We become like him, and we become his representatives, because he has called us to the wonderful task of showing his love to the world around us.

In preparation for this task, we can follow Jesus' example in seeking solitude. Jesus would often withdraw to a place where he could be alone and get close to God's heart.

It's such a busy world, not enough of us take time to be quiet before God. If we're not accustomed to it, it's difficult to plan the time and to train ourselves to do it. It's as though we say to God, "I'm so busy, I can't give you ten minutes, my life is so full."

Solitude is listening—listening to God. As we try to train ourselves to be quiet before God, it often helps to start off with a short prayer to God, "Speak to me," then wait quietly and listen, just as Jesus did, praying and listening to God.

We seek him, if we want to experience what Jesus promised.

An Everyday Obstacle

The problem of gossip pervades everyday life and is one of the top destroyers of community. It turns up everywhere in its hurtful opposition to God's love and commandment. Yet it presents an opportunity for a spiritual exercise that anyone can do, a practical way to change our hearts.

How about silence? Our morning prayer can ask God's help in refraining from saying any negative thing about anyone. Then if we feel compelled to say over lunch, "You can't believe what I heard," instead, as we remember our commitment, we develop a habit of silence in the face of gossip.

We can use our prayer life in asking God's help and guidance in dealing with the variety of sins inherent in our human nature. As we seek to tap the heart of God, the ultimate goal, what Jesus says will ultimately satisfy, will be abundant life in the Kingdom of God.

Don't Give Up

Another spiritual exercise that helps to transform our hearts, as many have experienced, is training in relation to assembly.

> Let us not give up meeting together, as some are in the habit of doing, but let us encourage one another.
>
> —Hebrews 10:25

Coming together to worship after serving and loving others can transform our lives. God is present where Christians gather together. As we enter our places of worship—a building, a garden, a service center, wherever or whatever that place may be, the first thing to say is, "It's all about God." Here's an opportunity for us to gather, worship, and refocus our attention from everything else in the world around us that's saying, "It's all about you."

In the worship service, we seek God first. There he can say things to us he won't say at any other time. The Holy Spirit prompts us and molds us in those moments. The commitment to meeting with others becomes a spiritual exercise, a spiritual training that transforms our hearts and connects us with God.

Trials and Hardships

How we deal with trials and hardships can strengthen our spirits and bring us closer to God. As we experience suffering and hardship, we may pray, "God take this away, take this away," but the Apostle Paul, who understood pain and suffering firsthand, teaches that,

> . . . we also rejoice in our sufferings, because we know that suffering produces perseverance; perseverance, character; and character, hope. And hope does not disappoint us, because God has poured out his love into our hearts by the Holy Spirit, whom he has given us.
> —Romans 5:3–5

When we experience that ache within, God often uses those times to provide moments of truth—of how he cares for us, how we matter to him, and how he can lead us through that darkness, even to pouring out more blessings on us. We can pray with confidence, "God, use this to mold me to be like you."

Countless testimonies are on record from people who have experienced job loss, financial ruin, devastating illness, broken relationships, every kind of pain. Yet through that suffering came a new and intimate knowledge of God's love and forgiveness, as God brought them through the pain to a life-transforming level of acceptance and peace that passes all understanding.

The Unlovable

Each of us has, or has had in our lives, someone very difficult to love. It's easy to obey God's commandment to love others when it's someone we love, but when it's someone we don't love, here comes the spiritual training.

Remember that God loves everyone. He loves us. He loves those people who want absolutely nothing to do with him. Even as he loves those who curse him, who use his name in cursing others, he says to us, "Do you want to have a heart like mine? Learn to love people who are unloving and unlovable."

Our spiritual training includes learning to love those unlovable people in our lives, to work at it, to try to bring them into our hearts. That's training that will bring our hearts in tune with God's.

Non-Christian Friends

Jesus spent time with people who were far from God. He went out of his way to seek them, invested his time, his love, and his wisdom with them. To follow his example we, too, will make sure we spend time with people in our lives who are far from God.

With my several good non-Christian friends, I find those relationships are very rich. They provide opportunities for me to love them, to invest in them, to understand God's heart toward them, and to pray for them.

The Kingdom Goal

King Solomon, famous for his wisdom, had the unlimited credit card. He could and did purchase anything he could lay his eyes on. When he had it all, he said,

> Yet when I surveyed all that my hands had done
> and what I had toiled to achieve,
> everything was meaningless, a chasing after the wind;
> nothing was gained under the sun.
> —Ecclesiastes 2:11

And here is Jesus who says to us, "If you want your life blessed, serve others."

> Now that I, your Lord and Teacher, have washed your feet, you also should wash one another's feet. I have set you an example that you should

do as I have done for you. I tell you the truth,
no servant is not greater than his master, nor is
a messenger greater than the one who sent him.
Now that you know these things, you will be
blessed if you do them.

—John 13:14–16

When we get up in the morning, we can pray, "God give
me an opportunity to bless somebody today. Give me an opportunity to serve somebody today." Or we can kneel, if that
is our custom, "God give me the strength to do this, to serve
others."

God wants us to have life and live it to its fullest. He shows
us the way, through the example of Christ, whose entire teaching was on loving and serving others. When we come to know
Christ, the power of the Holy Spirit, the power that raised
Christ from the dead, can make it possible for us to do that.
That's the power that enables us to truly love God with all our
souls and minds and to love our neighbors as ourselves.

Chapter Eleven

THE SHORTEST PRAYERS

The lumberyard looked as if it had been there for a hundred years, right out of the past, a rambling shack with cats sleeping all around, a dog, everyone in slow motion, and dusty products hanging on the walls.

While restoring an antique wooden power boat, I'd been looking for some Philippine mahogany, and finally found a lumberyard that had it. The owner took me up a ladder into his attic, where he had it stored.

I said, "Where do you get this stuff?"

"This has been in my family for years," he replied. "My grandfather bought a batch of it. I don't know what they were going to use it for, but it's here. How much do you need?"

As he was yanking out the planks and cutting them up, and I was loading them into the car, I thought of something else I had been needing for months. "Do you have a plug cutter for a number 10 screw?"

He said, "I think we have one back here." He shuffled around on the shelves, and he came out with the exact tool that I needed.

"I'll take it," I said.

It took him another thirty minutes to figure out how much to charge me for it. There wasn't a price tag in the whole place.

Finally, at home, as I looked more closely at the package, and read "1968 Stanley Corporation," I was struck with the realization that this tool had been hanging on a wall for 35 years. Here was this plug cutter that should have been in someone's tool box, that should have been used to make cabinets, flooring, and all kinds of carpentry projects, and should have had a wonderful 35 years of service, but here it was, never used.

To make matters worse, I couldn't use it either, because I found plugs already cut at Home Depot, and bought them for something like $1.39. So the plug cutter is still hanging around being unused.

> For we are God's workmanship, created in Christ Jesus to do good works, which God prepared in advance for us to do.
>
> —Ephesians 2:10

Over the years, on teaching on prayer and how to pray, I have heard others share with me some wonderful two-word prayers. As one friend would always say, "Just make it simple." Short but powerful, the response to them could be life changing. They have even been called "dangerous prayers."[4]

Use me

The first two-word prayer is "Use me." Some of us, in all our lives, have never been used by God. We've never prayed that prayer, "Use me."

There's nothing in my life that's been more exciting, more thrilling, and more fulfilling, than being used by God. Until you've experienced it, there's nothing like it. I can't describe to you how wonderful it is to know that God has used you when you have said, "Lord, use me."

God must look at some of us, thinking, "There's a usable tool, totally unused for ten, thirty, fifty years." We have a choice: we could be like that plug cutter hanging on a piece of cardboard, never having the adventure of being used, or we can ask God to use us.

Search me

The second of our two-word prayers comes from Psalm 139.

> Search me, O God, and know my heart;
>> test me and know my anxious thoughts.
> See if there is any offensive way in me,
>> and lead me in the way everlasting.
> —Psalm 139:23–24

David had started out praising and worshipping God, then, moving along, he realized that some people don't honor God. He reminds God of some wayward people he wants God to deal with. He continues to implore God to work in the lives of these other people, when suddenly he looks at his own life.

"Well, what about me? What about my life? I'd better pray for myself."

"Oh, God, search me. Turn the floodlights of the Holy Spirit on my life. See if there's anything in my life that can be a problem."

When we've seen others behaving in an ungodly manner, we're inclined to pray, "Oh, Lord, please deal with them. Show them your mercy. Show them who you are."

It's easy to pray for someone else, but when it comes to praying for ourselves, "Lord, work with *me*, search *me*," that's a different matter. A prayer like that can be life-changing, as David's must have been.

To those who have been investigating Christianity for some time, if you prayed, "Lord, search me," I think God would say, "Why are you hanging on the fence? Why are you still walking along the edge? Why don't you trust me? Why don't you take the step, and let's get about enjoying life together?"

It's usually fear that keeps us from giving our hearts to Christ, and from saying, "Lord, I need you in my life." We must know that God will address that fear when he turns the searchlight on our lives. It may be a fear of revealing some secret sins that we need to confess before him. Even before you pray, "Lord, search me," you know what the searchlight will expose. "Lord, you know where that searchlight's going—to that room that's locked up." Pray, "Search me," and God will forgive all that is past and change your life. God has a wonderful plan for each of our lives and, when we get to the end, we'll say, "Lord, thank you that I prayed a prayer like that." Remember, there's always a do-over with God.

Stretch me

There's another two-word prayer: "Stretch me."

As the New Testament church was being formed, the Romans were attacking the church, persecuting the early Christians. Yet, even in the midst of their persecution, the Christians continued to witness to their faith, praying,

> Now, Lord, consider their threats and enable your servants to speak your word with great boldness.
>
> —Acts 4:29

As I read that "stretch me" prayer, I wondered if I could have such strength under the circumstances they faced, or if I'd be calling for God's help, "Lord, send me an army, legions of angels, get me out of here!" But I don't think the first thing that would come into my mind would be, "Give me boldness."

Yet there were these Christians, praying for boldness as they faced persecution, and, as we know, they received strength and continued to love and share boldly about who Jesus Christ was.

Some of us need to be stretched in everyday situations, in our everyday lives. We can pray through the fruits of the spirit and ask the Lord to stretch us in each one of those virtues.

> . . . the fruit of the Spirit is love, joy, peace, patience, kindness, goodness, faithfulness, gentleness and self-control.
>
> —Galatians 5:22–23

I'm always in a rush, so a checkout line at Wal-Mart has me praying, "Lord, stretch me in my patience in this situation." I can remember my experience of trying to purchase a package of double A batteries at our local Home Depot. The only available checkouts were three self-checkout machines. Due to the newness of this method of checkout, the lines were extremely slow. Each line had six to eight people. I needed only a few minutes to check out my little package of batteries, only to discover that my item didn't scan.

So I tried to scan it again, and this time it scanned it twice. The machine was now asking me to put the item back in the bag, thinking that I had two packages of batteries instead of one. It kept saying "Put item back in bag." I kept pressing "cancel, cancel," but it wouldn't cancel.

The line behind me was getting longer and longer, and I was getting frustrated. I could hear a small voice in my head saying, "Put the batteries down, and walk out," as the machine kept saying, "Put item back in bag."

People were now scowling and wondering why I wasn't putting the items back in the bag. Finally, a clerk came to my rescue and enabled me to check out. As I ran from the building in embarrassment, I could hear the machine saying, "Put item back in bag. Put item back in bag."

We find ourselves saying the prayer, "Stretch me," in a variety of situations. "Stretch me in my forgiveness." "Stretch me in the way that I deal with my anger." "Stretch me in my compassion."

Some of us need to be stretched in how we deal with people who are going through difficulties. As you're rushing through, with places to go, people to see, you cross paths with some-one who is going through a difficult time. You don't have time to stop and spend some time with him or her. This is exactly the time when you may need a prayer like, "Stretch me in my compassion," and to take a few moments out to listen and to meet that need if possible. You could surprise yourself with the answer to prayer and find that you weren't so busy that you couldn't stop and be available to that person.

Lead me

"Lead me" is another simple, two-word prayer. My whole life, since the day I came to know Christ, has been about God leading me this direction and that, in both large and small situations.

Christians talk about leadings, "God prompted me," "God moved me," "God nudged me." The Holy Spirit is moving in their lives and guiding them. The adventure of the Christian life is based on the concept of God leading. If you pray, "God lead me," he will lead you. As you get up in the morning and say, "Lord, lead me," he will lead you wonderfully.

This is the first day of the rest of your life. You have this day, and whatever's in front of it. Who knows how long it is? You can grab hold of the steering wheel of your life, and you can grip it as tightly as you want—God is not going to take it out of your hands. He's not going to pry your fingers off that steer-ing wheel. You can drive your own life if you wish. Or, you can let go, and say, "Lord, lead me."

I guarantee you, as I've experienced in my life, and I know it's true of many others, God will lead you. It's a wonderful, wonderful adventure.

But you must be willing to say, "Lord, lead me." I can't tell you what a difference praying a simple prayer like that, the first thing in the morning, will make in your life, "Lord, lead me today." And during the day, with every breath of your life, be sensitive to his leading.

Don't miss it. It's a wonderful part of the Christian experience. God will lead you. It's one of the wonderful mysteries of God, that God uses us to accomplish his purposes.

Chapter Twelve

WHY CORPORATE WORSHIP?

"Why can't I just worship God at the beach?"

"I can worship God fine on roller blades, going down the boardwalk."

"I can worship God just fine in the woods, in the park, with a backpack, walking, or riding my bicycle."

"Why do I need to come to church? Isn't it enough, just to be alone with God anywhere?"

Once I was washed overboard during a storm. As I went over the side, I grabbed something which turned out to be the antenna to our Loran. It's an electronic instrument to which you can plug in coordinates of a chart, and that will tell you wherever you want to go. With it, anyone can drive a boat. It will take you right to that spot, within feet or inches if you can get it set just right, even in complete darkness. It has now been replaced by a more accurate instrument called a GPS, but the Loran has to be constantly re-calibrated. After getting back in the boat, with the help of my wife and a boat pole, and for some time after that, I had trouble getting the Loran back to its usual accuracy, until one day I succeeded in calibrating it so it wasn't taking me ten miles off course.

Our faith often needs recalibrating. Life, like boating, is full of uncertainties. Not knowing what kind of storm, problem, or situation will come our way, we must find a way to adjust our faith to be prepared.

In fellowship with others in the body of Christ, we learn the value of doing life together. For only as we do it together can we truly reach maturity in Christ.

We come together to reorient, recalibrate, so we can be ready to handle what comes our way.

Previous chapters have dealt with worship as one of the aspects of prayer, the way that we respond to God, with all that we are, to all that he is.

As people ask me why we come to church, we consider what the author of Hebrews wrote,

> And let us consider how we may spur one another on toward love and good deeds. Let us not give up meeting together, as some are in the habit of doing, but let us encourage one another—and all the more as you see the Day approaching.
>
> —Hebrews 10:24–25

As people ask me why we should come to a worship service, we consider what the author of Hebrews wrote. The author says that we should make it a habit to come together for worship, because to do so is God's will for our lives. For some of us, that's not enough. We ask why God wills it.

Verses 19 and 21 explain that corporate worship helps us to remember the work of Christ on our behalf.

Dallas Willard explains the value of corporate worship: "In fellowship we engage in common activities of worship, study, prayer, celebration, and service with other disciples. This may involve assembling ourselves together in a large group or meeting with only a few. Personalities united can contain more of God and sustain the force of his greater presence much better than scattered individuals. . . . Because of this reciprocal nature within the corporate body of Christ, fellowship is required to allow realization of a joyous and sustained level of life in Christ that is normally impossible to attain by all our individual effort, no matter how vigorous and sustained. In it we receive the ministry of all the graces of the Spirit to the church."[5]

Throughout Scripture, whenever a major event was taking place, the people of God drew together in corporate worship. We read of several of these events, such as the Exodus in the Old Testament. Revelation 4 and 5 talks about worshipping a risen and victorious Savior.

The Exodus of the Israelites from Egypt, when God parted the Red Sea, and they all marched off toward the Promised Land, has been commemorated ever since as a time of corporate worship. These days, we celebrate the greatest event in the history of mankind—what Christ did for us on Calvary—his death, burial, and resurrection, as the Book of Hebrews recounts,

> Therefore, brothers, since we have confidence
> to enter the Most Holy Place by the blood of
> Jesus, by a new and living way opened for us
> through the curtain, that is, his body, and since
> we have a great priest over the house of God,
> let us draw near to God with a sincere heart in
> full assurance of faith. . . .
>
> —Hebrews 10:19–22

The Old Testament people worshipped God in a tabernacle, or temple, where they had a sense of God's actual presence in an interior portion of the tabernacle, called the "Holy of Holies," that was separated from the rest of the worshippers by a thick curtain. Once a year, the priest would enter the Holy of Holies and offer a sacrifice for the sins of the people in a ceremony accompanied by fear and trembling on the part of those present. If, for some reason, the priest was not sincere, they believed that God would destroy everyone. The atmosphere of tension can only be imagined.

The writer of Hebrews assures us that now, as we draw together to remember the work of Christ on our behalf, we remember that we can always have confidence to come before him boldly.

The metaphor of the thick curtain illustrates that a new and living way is open to us through the body of Christ. Verse 21 goes on to explain that we have a great priest, Christ, who is making intercessions for us. Not only do we have confidence to come before God, but now we have a Priest who is making intercessions for us. It's as though Jesus were looking down and saying, "There are people who are in need. I'll give them grace. . . . There are people who are failing, and I'll give them mercy. . . . There are people who are hurting, and I'll give them sympathy."

Every time we come together, it reminds us that we have a High Priest who is sympathetic and who provides mercy and grace for every one of us.

The passage from Hebrews speaks of the new relationship that Christ has opened up for us. Now God no longer has his back to us, but is facing us. We are reconciled with our holy God through the wonderful work of Christ in paying the price for our sins. From that time on, we gather together to remember Christ's work in our behalf.

The Communion service provides a further example of the reason we come together in worship. Jesus asked us always to remember him through Communion, remember his broken body and the spilling of his blood. There, at the Communion table, we remember his death on the Cross for us.

"The day of the Lord's Supper is an occasion of joy for the Christian community," wrote Bonhoeffer. "Reconciled in their hearts with God and the brethren, the congregation receives the gift of the body and blood of Jesus Christ, and, receiving that, it receives forgiveness, new life, and salvation."[6]

The writer of Hebrews is saying that we need to come together because our heavenly Father isn't retired. He's still the Chief Executive Officer and every time we gather together in worship, we're remembering his work and the impact that he's had on our lives. He asked us to take Communion in remembrance of him. It's important that we do so.

The writer of Hebrews goes on to say,

> Let us draw near to God with a sincere heart.
> . . . Let us hold unswervingly to the hope we
> profess, for he who promised is faithful. And
> let us consider how we may spur one another
> on toward love and good deeds. Let us not give
> up meeting together . . .
>
> —Hebrews 10:22–25

When we come together to remember the work of Christ in our behalf, he helps us to reorient our faith.

The writer of Hebrews goes on to say that not only does our faith need recalibrating, but also we need to receive encouragement from each other, and to provide encouragement to one another. The passage reminds us to hold fast to the hope we know is there.

We need to get a new grip on our hope, to be prepared for those times when we hit some problems, and when feelings of uncertainty arise: "Am I winning or am I losing?" In corporate worship, we realize that Christ is on our side.

> And let us consider how we may spur one an-
> other on toward love . . .
>
> —Hebrews 10:24

First Corinthians 13 reminds us that faith, hope, and love form the center of all that it means to be a Christian. And when we come together to remember the work of Christ on our behalf, our faith is recalibrated, our hope restored, and we are spurred on to love and good works.

During any given week, if I don't take care of sin in my life, it produces a whirlpool effect, as when things on the outside spin inward, and I become self-centered and self-focused. The reverse happens when I join with others in corporate worship. Then I'm reminded of the love of Christ on my behalf.

Corporate worship affects our understanding of Christian love. Even though we've had problems with loving other people—problems at work, with our marriages, or even problems in the car on the way to church—when we come together to remember the love that Christ has for us, we are empowered to love other people. Corporate worship spurs us on to loving others as Christ is loving to us.

As we consider what God's Word says about how important corporate worship is to our lives, it becomes not an option but a priority.

Worship as corporate prayer

Worship is about God. If we don't realize that it's all about God, all the planning, the ministry of songs, prayers, and readings fall on deaf ears.

Worship gets off track when it becomes casual, when it's not a priority in our lives. A good illustration of casual worship occurs in the Old Testament. The story begins with Solomon building a temple to God where he placed objects of great beauty and value, all to the honor and glory of God, for which his people had sacrificed, and where people came to worship.

In that ancient Near Eastern culture, as Solomon knew, the placement in the temple of objects of great value and beauty helped the people realize that only the best they could offer would honor the great God of Abraham, Isaac, and Jacob. As they realized that their worship service was all about God, the beauty of their surroundings directed their attention to who God is and to their walk with him.

But Solomon's son, Rehoboam, did not understand that concept. After his father's death, the young ruler did not provide the people with the same example of commitment and was casual in his worship. Even when Rehoboam needed God's help, as in times of conflict with other nations, though he would show up at the temple and pray for help, his attitude and his approach were casual.

In time, the Egyptians came in conquest, plundered the Temple, and carted away all its precious contents. At that point, we may give Rehoboam a little credit for his effort to reconstruct the holy place. He did not abandon the faith, nor did he start to worship false gods. He went ahead to repair and replace, but, as he did so, instead of using materials of the finest quality, as Solomon had done, he replaced with cheaper materials.

That account contrasts with what we see in Exodus. When Moses brought the people of Israel out of the wilderness, across the Red Sea, they came together to worship. Exodus sets the scene:

> The Lord said to Moses, "I am going to come to you in a dense cloud, so that the people will hear me speaking with you and will always put their trust in you. . . ." And the Lord said to Moses, "Go to the people and consecrate them today and tomorrow. . . ."
>
> —Exodus 19:9–10

> On the morning of the third day there was
> thunder and lightning, with a thick cloud over
> the mountain, and a very loud trumpet blast.
> Everyone in the camp trembled. Then Moses
> led the people out of the camp to meet with
> God, and they stood at the foot of the moun-
> tain. Mount Sinai was covered with smoke,
> because the Lord descended on it in fire. The
> smoke billowed up from it like smoke from a
> furnace, the whole mountain trembled violent-
> ly, and the sound of the trumpet grew louder
> and louder. Then Moses spoke and the voice of
> God answered him.
>
> —Exodus 19:16–19

There they were, the people of Israel up on the mountain, with the ground shaking, flashes of lightning, and claps of thunder filling the atmosphere, smoke everywhere.

At that moment, what if someone in the crowd of people had called out, "Whatever happened to the dancing girls? I liked the dancing girls." Or, "It's too loud. Can't God tone it down a little bit? The smoke is getting in my eyes."

"What's with the pyrotechnics? Didn't God tell someone that that stuff's dangerous?"

Or someone else might say, "I like quiet worship, the way we used to do it."

And from the front row comes another comment, "Hey Moses, give me a break. Three days! You said it would only be a day or so!"

No, that's not what happened, was it? Yet isn't that typical of our attitude sometimes?

Casual worship can be compared to just another thing that we do throughout the week. We go to work. We have some other appointments. We schedule some relaxation time. Finally we show up at church, one more thing to do, and without anticipation.

God doesn't change. God was there at the mountain, with the smoke, the fire, and thunder, and he's the same God we worship today in our church sanctuaries. Yet, for some of us it's, "Well, yes, I'll do that and five other things."

One day I said to my congregation, "I know some of you work really hard to get here. I know it's tricky. You have kids, all kinds of stuff is going on in your home before you get here. Just getting here is a miracle, isn't it? Just the fact that you showed up is huge. So that's understandable. But, when we come late, it's an attitude of being casual. 'I'll get there when I get there.' It's not something you're thinking about. To reach the full potential for worship, we need to start preparing for worship ahead of time."

I asked them to remember their courtship days.

"Those of you who can remember back when you used to date, and some of you who are still single. Some of us spent more time getting ready for the date than the date actually lasted, didn't we? How was that different than coming before God here this morning?"

I asked them to try to think ahead about the worship service, to plan, to anticipate.

"Try this: Before you go to bed on Saturday night, say to yourself, 'Tomorrow morning, I'm going to be with God. I'm going to worship him.' You'll be preparing your heart.

"Better yet, what if you come here and pray about what is going on, pray for those leading worship, pray for our band, pray for the sound team, pray for the people who are going to come and sit next to you, pray that your heart will be open? Imagine what would happen in terms of worship! Then it wouldn't be casual, would it?"

When we switch out of casual, to worshiping God in spirit and in truth, we find God's love in our own hearts, his passion for lost people, for the poor. We can be filled with God's joy as we focus on him, his forgiveness, his mercy, and his grace.

When we come in anticipation to meet him, he will meet us in worship, and then we'll be able to say with the psalmist,

> Sing the glory of his name;
> make his praise glorious!
> —Psalm 66:2

How about consumer-oriented worship? We live in a consumer-oriented society. We go to a restaurant and expect good service. If we don't receive good service, we'll complain about it, tell others about it. We're not going to go back to that restaurant, are we?

We go to a movie and expect that movie to entertain us. If we liked it, as we leave we say, "Hey, that was a great movie. That was worth the ten bucks," or whatever it cost to get in there.

We go to Wal-Mart, and if we don't have to stand in a long line to get out, we say, "That was good service."

But if we bring our consumerism to the church service, we start looking at worship as "what I get out of it." We critique the service, as though it were a movie, or a theatrical performance.

But the worship service is not a show, not a movie, not entertainment. It's not about whether it meets your need, whether you liked it or didn't like it. Worship is about God, and it is where you meet God.

All kinds of splits and difficulties arise when on the subject of worship. At a church in which I served, with all that happened there in an hour, we tried to offer alternatives so that as many people as possible could "come to the mountain" and meet God.

Another way that worship goes off track, is in being narrow, choosing which part of the service to participate in and in which part to turn their backs or fall asleep.

Perhaps they'll skip either the singing or the sermon or don't participate in Communion or remain silent when the group prays in unison. That's narrowness, and it's related to the concept of consumerism.

Chapter 4 of John's gospel tells of a time when the disciples had taken off to find lunch, Jesus having chosen not to join them. While they were gone, he started a conversation about worship with a Samaritan woman who had come to draw water from the well. She said, "My people worship over here, and the Jews worship over there." Jesus said, "I've come so that you might worship in spirit and truth." Then he said something quite remarkable: "God is looking for people who will worship him."

Twenty-five to thirty times a year, give or take, somebody would talk to me, and I'd say, "You missed the first part." They'd say, "Ah, I only come for the message!"

Now for the other side of it. From where I stood, I could see every seat and every individual in the entire sanctuary, except for one or two who would be hiding behind pillars. As I said to them one day:

> I can see everything from here, believe me. Don't think that if you're in the balcony, all the way back there, that I can't see you. When it's time for the message, I can see people doing grocery lists, reading the bulletin—how many times can you read the bulletin? Sometimes people are passed out. I'm like, what happened?

Someone would say, "I only came for the emotional part, the spirit part, I didn't come for the teaching part."

I'd say, "It goes both ways. There has to be a balance. When we're here for an hour, and we come to the mountain to meet God, it's about everything."

Or they would have their preferences as to the type of message. "I have to have it more expository," "I want more storytelling," or "I have to have it more personal." Whatever the case is, if you're in that narrow, selective mode, the rest of us need you to get something done with your heart to keep the whole thing balanced.

I'm not demonstrative. I rarely clap. In a congregation where everyone's clapping, someone will say, "Bob, why don't you clap?"

"I don't know. I was worshipping without clapping."

Was there an assumption that if you don't clap you're not worshipping? Where did that come from?

Or someone says, "Why don't you put your hands up?"

Well, I can do touchdowns too, and that's a great way to submit to God, and it's wonderful, but if there's a desire, perhaps subconscious, to bring attention to yourself, that's not right either. The act of raising the hands is a great way of saying, "Oh, God! I'm all yours," as long as you're not doing it to bring attention to yourself. Another time we can discuss more about etiquette related to worship.

It's not about style. It's not about clapping your hands or raising your hands or any other gesture, it's about how you're responding to him, isn't it?

The life story of every church contains great, memorable defining moments when the entire body of the church, members and friends, experiences together an outpouring of the Holy Spirit as they rejoice in God's indescribable blessing on them. These high points in a church's journey may occur at the groundbreaking for a new church building; at some service of dedication, Baptism, or Communion; in thanksgiving for a year just passed; or even at some unexpected moment. These are times when the congregation responds to God's blessings in praise and thanksgiving.

Wherever a congregation may be in its journey toward building God's Kingdom, if there is anything beautiful about that journey, it will not have been the work of human hands, but of God's. If there's anything beautiful about what God has yet to do in that journey, it will all be God's. God works in a wonderful way in people's hearts to accomplish his will. They will feel his support, his clear guidance through each decision during a project. His ways are higher than ours. He does things that no one else can do. He deserves all the praise and obedient worship as the giver of every good and perfect gift.

It's amazing to me when I meet people who are not involved with any church, but who say, "I really love God!" I don't think it's possible to be in a right relationship with God and not be a part of fellowship.

At some point in your own Christian journey, you will become aware of the Holy Spirit's working in your life, and, as you respond, leading you to a closer relationship with God, a yielding to God, and a church community, the body of Christ. There is joy in being joined to others within an environment of Christian love, to love and to be loved, in a deep level of fellowship, worshipping, giving thanks, and giving praise, as you experience the true community that is a fully functioning body of Christ.

Then, you too will find the joy of worship in community, like the thousands of brand new Christians in those spirit-filled early days of the New Testament church, led by Peter and the apostles,

> ". . . everyone was filled with awe . . . they continued to meet together in the temple courts. They broke bread in their homes and ate together with glad and sincere hearts, praising God . . ."
>
> —Acts 2:43,46–47

APPENDIX

The following appendix contains a selection of personal and corporate prayers that I have offered during church worship services. These may be helpful at times when you find it difficult to know how or what to pray. You may even find it difficult to want to pray. These prayers may help you to push through those cloudy times in your life.

Over the centuries, Christians have relied on written prayers and found great personal connection with God through prayers written by others. Remember Jesus' response to the disciples, when they asked him how to pray? He gave them a prayer to pray, saying to them, "Pray like this. . . ." This gives us the idea that you could pray his exact prayer or that you could pray prayers that are in a similar manner as the famous Lord's Prayer. My personal tradition comes from being raised as an Episcopalian. Part of our corporate worship was to pray prayers that were already prewritten. Over the centuries, Christians have been doing exactly that, especially at times when they are facing troubled waters, and finding it helpful in drawing close to God.

CORPORATE PRAYERS

The first condition, which makes it possible for an individual to pray for the group, is the intercession of all the others for him and for his prayer. How could one person pray the prayer of the fellowship without being steadied and upheld in prayer by the fellowship itself?[7]

—Dietrich Bonhoeffer

FOR THE YOUTH MINISTRIES OF THE CHURCH AWAY ON A RETREAT

Heavenly Father, we ask that you would bless all our youth ministries, the Junior High, High School, and the Career ministries, who are away on retreat, studying, looking at your Word, and trying to determine your will for each of their own lives. Thank you for ____, their leader. We pray that you would continue to bless him, especially at this time while they have their own worship service away from us, but still as a part of us in the body of Christ. Grant them a sense of your presence during this time together and a safe trip home. In the name of our Savior, Jesus Christ. Amen.

FOR COMMITMENT TO PRAYER

Father, we thank you for your hand on our lives. We pray that as we move forward from this place that you would lead us to a deeper relationship with you, a deeper commitment to prayer, in Christ's name. Amen.

FOR THE HOLY SPIRIT'S PRESENCE

Father, we are so aware of your love, how you care so much for us, and that you want us to have all that you can provide for us. Help us to understand with clarity what it means to be filled with the Spirit, how we should act on what the Holy Spirit has for us, committing daily to you, and continually giving ourselves to you. I pray that we would be people that would be known for that, that we would walk in the Spirit and be filled with the Spirit. In Jesus' name I pray and ask these things. Amen.

FOR AUTHENTICITY IN WORSHIP

Father, we want to be a church that truly worships you in spirit and in truth. You look for people who will worship you, and we want to be those people. We want to worship you. Help us to do that in a way that's glorifying and honoring to you. In Christ's name. Amen.

FOR GOD'S PROTECTION

Heavenly Father, sometimes it's difficult for us to realize that you are ever present. We get caught up in the pressures of our own lives, and we fail to see you as you are, ever concerned, ever watching over us, protecting us, guiding us, directing us. Help us to understand your love and protection so that we might face the world we live in with great hope and confidence. We need your security, and we pray for your blessing on us that we would grow in willingness to trust and willingness to step out, realizing the help and strength that comes from you. In the name of our Savior, Jesus Christ. Amen.

FOR PEACE

Heavenly Father, you have asked us to pray for peace, to beseech you for right relationships among all people. As we think of the situation in the Middle East, we are so concerned, and we long to see peace delivered from your hand, that you would do a miracle there. We pray that you would guide the leaders, for all who are petitioning for peace, that they would have wisdom and that you would work through them. In the name of our Savior, Jesus Christ. Amen.

FOR OUR ENEMIES

Heavenly Father, you have commanded us to pray for our enemies. We think of those who wish to do us harm, and we pray that you would work in their lives that they might surrender and turn away from this conflict. We pray for them that, by your hand, good may triumph over evil. In the name of our Savior, Jesus Christ. Amen.

FOR AN AIRPLANE PILOT

Heavenly Father, we think of (our friend) who is flying at this time, and ask that you would protect him, give him wisdom, give him strength, that he might be wise in every decision that he makes for the safety of himself and the other people who are on his plane. In the name of our Savior, Jesus Christ. Amen.

FOR A MINISTER SEEKING EMPLOYMENT

Heavenly Father, we commit to your leading (our friend) as he searches for a pastorate in a place where he can use his gifts and abilities in your service. These are difficult and stressful days for him and his family, when they don't know where they're going, and where you are leading them. We ask that you would protect him and his family, giving them confidence to know that you are guiding and directing them, and that this is just another step in the adventure of walking with you. In the name of our Savior, Jesus Christ. Amen.

FOR THOSE SEEKING EMPLOYMENT

Heavenly Father, for those that are still searching for employment, this has been a difficult year. We ask that you would give grace, confidence, and determination that they would not lose hope but that they would be strengthened as they continue to look to you for your guidance and direction. In the name of our Savior, Jesus Christ. Amen.

FOR THOSE NEEDING INTERCESSION

Heavenly Father, we hold before you all who are in need of prayer. You know all who need a special intercession in their lives, people who are hurting, experiencing depression, bereavement, illness, sorrow, and troubles of many kinds, and we pray that you would meet those needs. In the name of our Savior, Jesus Christ. Amen.

FOR A VACATION BIBLE SCHOOL

Heavenly Father, we pray for the programs where children can have the wonderful experience of learning about you. At this time, we ask that you would bless our Vacation Bible School program, five days of intensive opportunity to share the knowledge and love of Christ through music, through your Word, and through people's involvement with children. We pray that this program, where so many people have had their first contact with the truth of the Gospel, as it has in the past, year after year, will continue to communicate to this community the love that we have for you. We thank you for all the workers, and we ask your blessing on them, on all the people who have taken off from work, changed their schedules, and made sacrifices for this special week. Bless them to overflowing as they have this opportunity to be involved in other people's lives. In the name of our Savior, Jesus Christ. Amen.

FOR A VACATION BIBLE SCHOOL JUST CONCLUDED:

Heavenly Father, we thank you for the wonderful work of this ministry. We think of the kids that sang and the incredible week that we had—hundreds and hundreds of kids. Over a hundred adults were involved, and we all benefited. We all sensed that you were working and ministering through us, and we thank you for that. For the week just past, we praise you and thank you, in the name of our Savior, Jesus Christ. Amen.

FOR THOSE ON VACATION

Heavenly Father, for those who are away on vacation, we ask that you would bless them and their families, that these would be relaxing times but also bonding times for children and parents, wonderful opportunities for strengthening the family units. We need a lot of that today, as we again pray that you would strengthen each of our families. In the name of our Savior, Jesus Christ. Amen.

FOR FRIENDSHIP, ON READING THE STORY OF DAVID AND JONATHAN

Heavenly Father, how thankful we are for your Word, where we read of the friendship between David and Jonathan. The story barely touches the surface of such a deep relationship, but how encouraging it is to realize that same potential is there for each of us, friends brought together by you. We thank you for the love of many brothers and sisters, loving and caring for one another, impossible to describe, and that we are a part of it. In the name of our Savior, Jesus Christ. Amen.

FOR CHRISTIANS IN FOREIGN LANDS

Heavenly Father, we think of people in Indonesia, across the world. We ask that you would bless that congregation of believers who for the first time has finally been permitted to build a building where they can worship. We pray that you would enable their need for chairs to be met, through the offerings raised in our Vacation Bible School program, so that our children would be able to reach out to the children in that congregation, as they spread the love of Christ across the ocean. In the name of our Savior, Jesus Christ. Amen.

THAT WE MAY HEAR GOD'S VOICE

Heavenly Father, we want to be a people who listen to you. May we not be led astray, but may we hear your voice and what you are saying to us. Help us to recognize your voice over others, and may we be a people who are known for our relationship with you. In the name of our Savior, Jesus Christ. Amen.

FOR VICTORY IN TEMPTATION

Heavenly Father, we know that for some the subject of Satan's influence seems hard to grasp. We don't like to talk about it. And yet we know that it's a reality, an enemy who wishes to destroy us. We pray that you would help us to be alert Christians, that we would be aware of Satan's power and activity, that we would be wise, victorious over temptation, as we rely on you. In the name of our Savior, Jesus Christ. Amen.

FOR RESISTANCE TO TEMPTATION

Heavenly Father, often the words that we hear seem so right: "Don't be overcommitted," "Don't be too zealous," "Back off, just be mildly committed." Help us to ignore Satan's cunning words so that we may press forward and experience all that you have for us—a wonderful, abundant Christian experience. Help us to have wisdom to know your will for us, to be careful about denying legitimate relationships, feelings, and recreation. In the name of our Savior, Jesus Christ. Amen.

FOR THOSE SERVING THE POOR

Heavenly Father, we pray for those who are working in the Soup Kitchen to feed people who are hungry, and who are washing dishes this morning, that the reality of the cross will burn richly in their hearts as they serve others. Then for ourselves, as we have opportunities to serve others, to give back again some part of that which you did for us, may we be reminded over and over again of the visible experience of your love for us. In the name of our Savior, Jesus Christ. Amen.

IN PREPARATION FOR COMMUNION

Heavenly Father, we come in humility, realizing there is nothing about us that deserves your grace, but only because of your amazing love do you approach us. Father, we are taking part in Communion this morning, as you instructed us, so that we will never forget that it's all about you. You did it all, and we are only miserable sinners apart from your grace. Thank you for your love and for what you have done for us through your Son Jesus Christ our Lord. Amen.

FOR OUR SPIRITUAL GROWTH

Heavenly Father, may we always live a life that's pleasing to you, to move toward being your fully devoted followers. We want to be holy and true before you. We pray that we may continue to follow the example of Christ himself, and the disciples who followed him, even those, today, who are in leadership here at our church. We know that the way that we live affects so many other people. We're thankful for the truths that you've taught us, things that you've changed in our lives. Here, too, at this church, how you've been changing and molding this body. It's exciting to realize that each day, just as we are individually changed, the body of Christ changes. We're not the same as we were three months ago. We're not the same as we were six months ago. As we move forward in our faith and in our love for you, we're thankful in the realization that we, as a congregation, are maturing, becoming more and more holy and perfect before you, so that one day we can come before you, holy and blameless. In the name of our Savior, Jesus Christ. Amen.

FOR A FILLING OF THE HOLY SPIRIT

Father, you are a loving God, and you care so much for us. You want us to have all that you have available for us. Help us to understand with clarity what it means to be filled with the Spirit. I pray that we would act on what the Holy Spirit has for us. I pray that we would be people who would be known for that, that we would walk in the Spirit and be filled with the Spirit. I pray that you would speak to each one of us in love, touching our hearts, and filling our hearts with your Holy Spirit. In Jesus' name. Amen.

FOR FAITHFULNESS IN CORPORATE WORSHIP

Father, we ask that you would touch our hearts toward a fuller understanding of how important corporate worship is, with other believers struggling through the same kinds of problems, so we can come together once a week and have our faith recalibrated and the sincerity of our love for others strengthened, as we learn to be your fully devoted followers. In Christ's name, we ask these things. Amen.

THAT WE MIGHT TAKE ON CHRIST'S NATURE

Heavenly Father, we are thankful for all that you have given us. Teach us to be giving people, to reflect your very nature, following your example, in the basic quality of giving. In the name of our Savior, Jesus Christ. Amen.

FOR OPENNESS IN COMMUNICATION

Heavenly Father, we thank you that we can talk openly and honestly about the things that are so important in everyday life, things like money, our personal walk with you, and how to know you personally. We thank you for the privilege we have here to teach the whole Word of God. In the name of our Savior, Jesus Christ. Amen.

FOR SEEKERS AND DOUBTERS

Heavenly Father, we pray for those who come as our guests, who are not yet Christians. Perhaps they're holding out, trying to get more information, putting it all together, deciding whether they really want to know you and serve you and that you would be a part of their lives. Some are thinking, "If I give my life to Christ, I'm going to lose everything. I'll lose my personality, I'll lose my freedom, I'll become something different, something that I don't want to be." We pray for all seekers, and we ask that you would touch their hearts, help them to realize that you help us to be complete, to be free indeed. To receive the perfect freedom that you provide, all we need to do is call on your name and ask you to forgive us for our sins. You have promised that, if we do so, you would forgive us and make us children of God. Enable doubters and seekers to pray a very simple prayer: "Lord forgive me for my sins. Come into my life and be my Lord." We pray that you would guide them, lead them to making a wonderful, joyous decision of knowing you. In the name of our Savior, Jesus Christ. Amen.

FOR THOSE INVESTIGATING CHRISTIANITY

Heavenly Father, we pray for those who are visiting this morning, those who are investigating Christianity, that they would test the truths taught here, recognizing the value of our spiritual diversity. May we all seek you in spirit and in truth. In the name of our Savior, Jesus Christ. Amen.

FOR AN ANNUAL MEETING

Heavenly Father, this is a difficult time in the history of mankind to raise a family. Many aspects of society are, in some sense, running against the practice of our Christian faith. Help us to be constantly aware of the importance of our role, and may we be wise in taking advantage of the resources we have. We ask that you would bless our meeting. May it be one of great rejoicing and excitement about the work of the church over the past year, as we have shared your love with this community, and as we make plans for next year that could impact the future of the world. In the name of our Savior, Jesus Christ. Amen.

FOR THOSE NOT PRESENT

Heavenly Father, we pray for those who aren't here this morning, those who are away traveling, the young people on their retreat, and those who are unable to make it because of the weather. We ask that your blessing be upon them as they worship at home or wherever they are. In the name of our Savior, Jesus Christ. Amen.

FOR ENCOURAGEMENT TO REPENTANCE

Heavenly Father, we pray that we would be drawn to the cross of Christ that brings an answer to the issue of sin. We pray that there would be a response of repentance from all of us. In the name of our Savior, Jesus Christ. Amen.

FOR THE OFFERING

Father, I pray for every one of us here that we would learn to be giving people—to learn the discipline of tithing, to learn the joy of giving, to respond to the Holy Spirit's guidance—that our giving will be done in love, as you have loved us. We ask this in Christ's name. Amen.

FOR MOMENTS OF TRUTH

Heavenly Father, we thank you for the moments of truth that you bring to each of us. Those moments come when we least expect them, sometimes when the stuffing gets knocked out of us or when it comes through a carefully placed Christian or whether it's in the form of a blessing that overflows us. Help us, we pray, to be open to your still, small voice that brings a moment of truth that can change our lives. In the name of our Savior, Jesus Christ. Amen.

FOR DELIVERANCE FROM THE SIN OF WILLFULNESS

Heavenly Father, "Thy will be done" is our prayer. May it be a reality from now on, consistently and regularly. We know we can expect moments of temptation but that we'll say, "Your will be done," as Jesus taught us: "Thy Kingdom come, thy will be done." Bless us, change us, help us to understand that the course of our lives depend on that simple prayer. In the name of our Savior, Jesus Christ. Amen.

FOR RECOGNITION OF GOD'S PLAN FOR OUR LIVES

Heavenly Father, help us to recognize the unique plan for each of our lives. We know that comes first from a relationship with you, to know you personally and be led by you along the way. May we be found, at the ends of our lives, having followed your plan well and faithfully. In the name of our Savior, Jesus Christ. Amen.

FOR SPIRITUAL DIVERSITY

Heavenly Father, we thank you that you did not make us all the same. Every one of us is wired up differently, and we all have different gifts, different passions, and different ways of relating to you. Help each of us to recognize our own unique way of responding to your spiritual truths, and help us to find how to have a more consistent walk with you. In the name of our Savior, Jesus Christ. Amen.

FOR FORGIVENESS

Heavenly Father, we thank you that you come into our lives and change us, forgiving us for our sins. We can always find ourselves at your feet, with great gratitude, adoration, and devotion to you because of what you've done. May we love you in humility. Only in your hands, and in reflection of your love, can our lives count. In the name of our Savior, Jesus Christ. Amen.

FOR STRENGTH IN TIME OF TROUBLE

Heavenly Father, we thank you for the truth. Sometimes we need a wake-up call. Maybe this is a wake-up call for each one of us. We've seen your grace pour out all over this country and on our lives, even in our tenderness this morning. Some of us haven't been here in a long time, and we are here this morning saying, "OK, Lord, I need answers." Lord, give us answers. May we draw close to you and find your comfort and your love. May we communicate that to our friends who need to hear about your love. In the name of our Savior, Jesus Christ. Amen.

ON REMEMBERING TERRORIST ATTACKS

Heavenly Father, we remember that day when our hearts were rocked with the greatest tragedy that has faced modern history right here on our own soil. We pray for the many families that are out there today without a father, without a mother, without a son or a daughter. Jesus reminded us over and over again to mourn with those who mourn. We mourn with them at their loss. We remember that we need to continue to pray for our leaders, our president, and others who are making decisions on this war against terrorism. We pray for our soldiers who are on the field today, and we pray for those families that have lost loved ones in suicide and terrorist attacks. We also pray for national leaders in other countries, that they would have great wisdom to do what is right and not in revenge. We pray for peace in our land and in our world and that we would remember again afresh at this time those things that you spoke to us about individuality. That our faith would be rekindled and made anew, that our commitment would be strong. In the name of our Savior, Jesus Christ. Amen.

IN RESPONSE TO TRAGEDY

Heavenly Father, we know that we live in a world that's corrupt. There's heartache and disappointment and sadness in all the rest of that's around us. We don't know what the next year's going to hold. We don't know what it will mean for us as a congregation. We pray that you will teach us to live every moment, moment by moment, with you, with eternity in view. May we live as people of hope. In the name of our Savior, Jesus Christ. Amen.

IN REMEMBRANCE OF TRAGEDY

Heavenly Father, we give you thanks for your constant love toward us and your healing power on our lives. Although we remember the time when our community and our world was rocked by evil, yet throughout these years, we have seen your faithfulness. Again we remember, and will not forget, that you are always with us. In the name of our Savior, Jesus Christ. Amen.

FOR COMPASSION ON READING JOHN 8:1

Heavenly Father, we looked at this passage this morning, and we realize it was over 2,000 years ago this woman found herself standing there before you thinking, "How did I end up here?" None of us want to say those very words. Yet we pray that we would take the necessary step. Because sin unchecked goes deeper and deeper. We hold stones in our hands. In the first moment, we are critical about this, critical about that, negative, angry, and we throw stones. We pray that we would be people of compassion, especially here at our church where we know the truth that you came to set us free. May we model your love and your compassion. May today also be the day that we make a decision about the sin in our lives. In the name of our Savior, Jesus Christ. Amen.

FOR A RIGHT ATTITUDE

Heavenly Father, we pray for your guidance, that we may be hopeful, optimistic, other-oriented, God-honoring people. It's not easy, because often our attitudes are exactly the opposite. It takes self-discipline, self-leadership, and perseverance. May we strive to accomplish that, for your glory. In the name of our Savior, Jesus Christ. Amen.

FOR THE RIGHT USE OF OUR GIFTS AND TALENTS

Heavenly Father, it would be easy to walk through these doors today and say, "Not me. I'm too busy. Too much on my plate." Help us not to miss the Christian life. Help us not to be deceived by tempting alternatives. Help us to hear your voice more clearly than we have ever heard it before. Help us not to blow you off one more time. In the name of our Savior, Jesus Christ. Amen.

FOR COURAGE, A WOMAN'S PRAYER

Heavenly Father, we stand here on Mother's Day asking your guidance that we may be women of character. There are times when we need to step up in courage, and ask you where you're leading us. If we trust you and move ahead in confidence, you have a great work for us to do. In the name of our Savior, Jesus Christ. Amen.

FOR HELP IN ESTABLISHING PRIORITIES

Heavenly Father, your words are so clear. How easy it is to invest our whole lives in that which rusts, rots, or can be stolen. How logical and truthful it is to realize that we can invest in the greatest portfolio that anyone can invest in and that's in eternity, guaranteed by you. May we always recognize the love you have for us and what Christ did for us, so that we might have eternal life. In the name of our Savior, Jesus Christ. Amen.

FOR TEACHERS

Heavenly Father, we ask your blessing on those who have that gift and ability to be teachers. May they be encouraged and strengthened daily. And then for all of us, because we all teach in some way, in our own personal lives, with our families, with our friends, and in our work, may we be found as effective leaders, with your blessing. In the name of our Savior, Jesus Christ. Amen.

TO BE EXTENSIONS OF GOD'S GRACE

Heavenly Father, you said that for every one of us who knows you, we would be like a light to the world. The world that we live in today needs a lot of light. In the many different ways there are for us to be a light to the communities around us, in our own neighborhoods, among our friends, and in our workplaces, our prayer is for your help and your blessing on us as we find appropriate ways to communicate your love. In the name of our Savior, Jesus Christ. Amen.

FOR GOD'S INTERVENTION IN HEALING FOR A CHILD DURING LONG ILLNESS, AND FOR HIS MOTHER

Heavenly Father, we come humbly before you with many requests for healing among our congregation. First, we ask that you would open our hearts, our ears, and our eyes to your truth, that you would help us to be sensitive to your leading to us as a congregation and to each of us individually.

Then, Lord, we ask for your intervention on behalf of Daniel. We have been so grateful that, as his mother has told us, she couldn't have gone through this without your presence, without your grace comforting her and providing for her. Even for us, as a congregation or as individuals, knowing the situation, I don't know how we would have been able to press through without knowing that you were working through each of those steps, working through the doctors there on Friday morning. Lord, we ask that this operation would finally start a recovery process for Daniel, that there would be no more problems and that he might recover and be as any other little boy, enjoying life without concern of a bruise or a bump.

Then Lord we pray for Daniel's mom that you would give her strength there in the hospital. Help her not to be fatigued, and we pray that she might be strong, and that you'd give her rest, even as she has to sleep in a chair, Lord, we ask that you would strengthen her there.

Then, Father, again we appeal to you on behalf of each one of us, that as we seek you, we might truly know you. We ask these things in the name of the Father, the Son, and the Holy Spirit. Amen.

PERSONAL PRAYERS

It boils down to this: If you are willing to invite God to involve himself in your daily challenges, you will experience his prevailing power—in your home, in your relationships, in the marketplace, in the schools, in the church, wherever it is most needed.[8]

—Bill Hybels

A FATHER'S PRAYER

Father, I struggle every day with how to be a good Dad, how to provide the gifts for my children that really count, to spend time with my children, and to help them to grow in their love for you and in their journey to maturity. Help me to be a father who affects my children in a positive way. In Christ's name. Amen.

FOR A LIFE PLEASING TO GOD

Father, I've seen you working and moving in my life, and helping me to live in a way that's pleasing to you. Yet it may take the rest of my life for you to transform me. Thank you that the Holy Spirit is busy at work, prompting and molding me, so that eventually, through my life, I might communicate to others the truth of what the Christian life is really all about. I pray in Christ's name. Amen.

FOR CONSISTENCY IN PRAYER

Father, I confess to being so busy in my life that I keep forgetting to take time to spend in prayer with you, having a relationship with you, speaking with you. I don't want to wait till there's a bump in the road, when I know I'll call out to you in a panic. Help me open the avenue to you so that I can be more consistent in my prayer life, experiencing afresh your peace that passes all understanding. I ask this in your holy name. Amen.

CONFESSION

Father, I know that I am a sinner and that I need to turn from that to become simply and humbly a follower of you. I ask that what Jesus did on the cross be applied to my life and to my sin. I invite Christ into my life right now. In Jesus' name. Amen.

ON STUDYING THE BIBLE

Father, I thank you for your Word. Sometimes it comes across as encouraging and uplifting, though sometimes it cuts. As I've worked on this, I've been challenged to the very core of my soul on what it means to be a listener, that I would mature, that I would have ears to hear, eyes to see the truth, and a mouth that speaks truth. It's my desire, in every aspect and every sense, to be a true seeker. In Christ's name. Amen.

IN THANKS FOR GOD'S LOVE

Father, how thankful I am that you loved me even when I didn't know you and didn't love you. You were willing to give your life so that I might have salvation. I remember how important it is to trust and how you trusted in the heavenly Father, even to the point of dying on the cross, realizing that this would bring men and God back together. Thank you that I am personally reconciled to you through Jesus. I pray in Christ's name. Amen.

IN THANKS FOR GOD'S LOVE

Gracious heavenly Father, I thank you for your love. I don't want to forget what you have done for me. I think back to that moment when I understood for the very first time what it means to have a relationship with you, and I asked you to come into my life, and how that has radically changed the course and direction of my life. That one defining moment changed everything in my life. I pray, Father, that you would continue to remind me on a daily basis of the whole meaning of grace. In Jesus' name. Amen.

FOR A NEW YEAR

Heavenly Father, I pray that you would help me to bring the life-changing understanding of your grace to my friends, to my neighbors, to my family. I want to be a fully devoted follower of Christ. Whatever it takes, Lord, use me. Thank you for the year just past. Thank you that the blessings in my life are all possible because of you. I give you the glory and thank you. Thank you, Jesus. Amen.

FOR A CLOSER WALK WITH CHRIST

Heavenly Father, I need your Holy Spirit to help me be more compassionate, more dedicated to service, more loving of other people. Lord, I pray that I might follow your example in these areas and move closer to you day by day, week by week, and year by year. Help me to do this, because I believe it is your wish to be closer to me. In Jesus' name. Amen

FOR HELP TO MANAGE ANGER

Heavenly Father, I know you call me to rightly handle and manage my anger. I pray that you will enable me to start by having just one week where I can manage my anger, so that this week will be a new week for me, that I won't respond the way I have in the past. I pray in Christ's name. Amen.

AS A WILLING GIVER

Heavenly Father, as I take part in the offering, I ask that you would continue to help me to see that this is worship. It is not just a collection. It it not dues or a debt that I owe. Lord, you have provided wealth, and I'm just a steward. Money doesn't have a hold on me. Thank you, thank you for your wonderful blessing on my life. In Jesus' name. Amen.

AS A HESITANT GIVER

Heavenly Father, sometimes I find it tough to make an offering. Yet I know that as much as you talked about heaven and hell, you talked more about what I should do with my resources. I know that how I handle my resources says a lot about who I am, my character, my life, and my devotion to you. I need to remember how you always provide for us, and I ask for your leading and your direction so that I will become truly devoted to you and experience the blessing that comes from that. In Christ's name. Amen.

FOR FREEDOM FROM DEBT

Heavenly Father, I need to experience the full benefit of freedom in Christ. I know it begins by being morally free, by receiving you as my Savior and experiencing what it means to be a child of God. I know the steps to take to be free from debt, to lift that burden, and to make decisions that will lead me to have a right relationship with you. In Christ's name. Amen.

COMMITMENT

Lord Jesus, Son of the Father, I need you as my Savior. Forgive me of my sins. Come into my life. For I want the promise of John 1:12, to be a child of God. In Jesus' name. Amen.

FOR FULL DEVOTION

Heavenly Father, I need to stop holding you at arm's length but to express my full devotion to you in plain words, right now. It's in my heart to say that I truly have given my life to you. I believe that Jesus is the Son of God. I believe that he has authority over my life. I believe that he died for the forgiveness of my sins. I believe that he rose from the dead to give me life forever. Forgive me of the wrong things I have done. Create in me a clean heart. Teach me to obey you, to follow you the rest of my life. I pray in Christ's name. Amen.

IN REPENTANCE

Heavenly Father, it's my heart's desire to repent. Search me. Turn the floodlights on in my life. You have free access to go any place you want. Do anything you want. Go to any room, any closet, look under any bed. Whatever it is, Lord, search me. I pray in Christ's name. Amen.

FOR GOD'S LEADING

Heavenly Father, I don't want to miss out on the adventure of the Christian life. I want that wonderful experience of being led by you. Nudge me. Guide me. Lord, I know I've never heard an audible voice from you, but I pray that I will always feel you push and nudge and guide in my life in your marvelous way so that I will always experience what it means to be led by you. I pray in Christ's name. Amen.

FOR GUIDANCE

Lord, it's sobering to me to realize that I've been playing the wrong game. I know what I need to do. Help me, lead me to live my life wisely. In Jesus' name. Amen.

FOR RENEWAL

Heavenly Father, I seem to have drifted so far from you since making my original commitment to you. I want to renew my vows, to say again, Lord Jesus, I love you, and I want you in the center of my life. That is my prayer today. In Jesus' name. Amen.

IN A TIME OF DEPRESSION

Heavenly Father, you know the pain that's deep down, that causes me to act that way. You know I'm covering it with work . . . (exercise) (sleep) (deal making) (many other things) to cover the pain. I need to experience what it means to be free from depression, and to experience life in its fullness. Father I pray that you will touch my heart so that I might truly be free and experience all that you have for me. In Jesus' name. Amen.

ON BEING SINGLE

Heavenly Father, it's tough to run against the stream. It's tough to be the odd (man) (woman) out. Yet, I know that the Holy Spirit will come to give me strength, courage, and determination to do what is right. For myself, and for others who are single, I pray that you would give us courage to live lives that are holy and pure before you. I pray in Christ's name. Amen.

FOR RELEASE FROM THE POWER OF MONEY

Heavenly Father, it's crucial that I understand the priorities in my life, whether it's you or something else. I pray that you would touch my heart and help me to realize where I am in that process. I believe that my decision relating to that will change the course of my life, and I ask your blessing on my choices. I pray in Christ's name. Amen.

FOR SPIRITUAL RENEWAL

Heavenly Father, I truly desire to be in a right relationship with you. Yet, somehow I sense that things aren't quite right. I'm in a spiritual slump. Show me where I'm out of kilter, out of balance spiritually. I will try to correct the problems in my life so that I may be restored to a renewed relationship with you. I pray that you would use me in a way that brings peace and love and direction in my life, so that I might experience the fullness of what it means to know and walk with you. In Jesus' name. Amen.

ON FACING A DIFFICULT TASK

Heavenly Father, I'm facing something that scares me. Yet I know that you're faithful. You made a covenant with your people that said you're one hundred percent for us. I trust you. I believe you will catch me and protect me. I need to do this. I will do it knowing that you'll be faithful this time, as you are in every situation. Thank you for being beside me in this venture. I pray in Christ's name. Amen.

FOR WISDOM IN MANAGING FINANCES

Heavenly Father, as I think through the issues of my tithing and my commitments, today is the day I will make it right, to take steps to manage my financial resources in a wise and God-honoring way. I pray for guidance in making wise decisions in this area of finances. I pray in Christ's name. Amen.

TO BE USED BY GOD

Heavenly Father, here I am. Use me. I want to be a usable tool in your hands and for your workmanship so that my life from this day forward will be a life of wonderful adventure, realizing that I was used by you to advance your Kingdom here in a local church and through its mission, in our community and around the world. Lord, use me. In Jesus' name. Amen.

IN TIME OF SADNESS

Heavenly Father, you know the sadness of my heart. I remember from one of your parables how clearly you said that you are available, that you can hear us and that you want to respond. I thank you as I realize that you are right here. Thank you for your help. Thank you for being here. Thank you for your words of comfort. In Jesus' name. Amen.

FOR PURITY OF SPEECH

Heavenly Father, I often forget that my words influence everyone with whom I come into contact. I pray for your help to overcome a habit of careless speech, that's even sometimes disrespectful of you. From now on, from the moment that I open my eyes in the morning to the moment that I close them at night, may no unwholesome word come out of my mouth. I pray in Christ's name. Amen.

FOR RENEWAL

Heavenly Father, I seem to have drifted so far from you. Lord I want to renew my vows, to say again, Lord Jesus, I love you and I want you in the center of my life. This is my prayer today. In Christ's name. Amen.

ENDNOTES

1. Bonhoeffer, Dietrich, *Life Together*, translated, and with an introduction by John W. Doberstein. Copyright 1954 by Harper & Row, Publishers, 42–43.
2. Bonhoeffer, 73–75.
3. *It All Goes Back in the Box*, is the title of a sermon by John Ortberg, published by Willow Creek Association, 1994.
4. *Dangerous Prayers* is the title of a sermon series published by Willow Creek Association, 1991–2001.
5. Willard, Dallas, *The Spirit of the Disciplines: Understanding How God Changes Lives*. Copyright 1988 by Dallas Willard. New York: HarperCollins, 1991, 186–187.
6. Bonhoeffer, 122.
7. Bonhoeffer, 63.
8. Hybels, Bill, with LaVonne Neff, *Too Busy Not to Pray: Slowing Down To Be With God*, InterVarsity Press, 1998, 2d ed., 15.

RESOURCES

Bonhoeffer, Dietrich, *Life Together*, translated, and with an Introduction by John W. Doberstein. Copyright, 1954, by Harper & Row, Publishers.

Burr, Richard A., with Arnold R. Fleagle, *Developing Your Secret Closet of Prayer*, Christian Publications, Inc., 1998.

Hybels, Bill, with Lavonne Neff, *Too Busy Not to Pray: Slowing Down To Be With God*, InterVarsity Press, 1998.

Hybels, Bill, and Kevin Harney, *Prayer: Opening Your Heart to God*, Zondervan, 2005.

Lockyer, Herbert, *All The Prayers of the Bible, A Devotional and Expositional Classic*. Zondervan, 1959.

Murray, Andrew, *The Prayer Life*, Moody Press, 1989.

Phillips, E. Lee, *Prayers for Worship,* Baker Book House, 1979.

Redpath, Alan, *Victorious Praying: Studies in the Family Prayer,* Fleming H. Revell, 1957.

Stedman, Ray C., *Jesus Teaches on Prayer*, Word Books, 1975.

Warren, Rick, *The Purpose-Driven Life: What on Earth Am I Here For?* Zondervan, 2002.

Willard, Dallas, *The Divine Conspiracy: Rediscovering Our Hidden Life in God.* Foreword by Richard J. Foster; HarperCollins, 1998.

Willard, Dallas, *The Spirit of the Disciplines: Understanding How God Changes Lives.* HarperCollins, 1991.

Willow Creek Association, *The Journey: A Bible For Seeking God & Understanding Life.* Zondervan, 1996.

Willow Creek Association, sermons: Steve Gillen, *Dangerous Prayers, Part 2: God Search Me,* 2001; Stevens, Jarrett, *Dangerous Prayers, Part 3, God, Change Me,* 2001; Bill Hybels: *Dangerous Prayers, Part 4: Privilege of Prayer,* 1991; *Pray at Your Own Risk,* 1997. John Ortberg: *It All Goes Back in the Box,* 1994; *Moses: A Journey Towards God: Part 11: Intercessory Prayer,* 1997; *The Wonder of Worship, Part 1: Why Worship Matters,* 1998; *What Makes Prayer Powerful?* 1998; *The Wonder of Worship, Part 4: Worship as a Way of Life,* 1998. Nancy Ortberg: *Dangerous Prayers, Part 1: God Hear Me,* 2001.

INDEX